BETTER HOMES AND GARDENS®

New Decorating Book

A **Better Homes and Gardens.** Book
An Imprint of

BETTER HOMES AND GARDENS® MAGAZINE
Gayle Goodson Butler
Executive Vice President, Editor in Chief
Oma Blaise Ford
Deputy Editor, Home Design
Mike Belknap
Creative Director

BETTER HOMES AND GARDENS® NEW DECORATING BOOK
Editor: Paula Marshall
Contributing Editors: Jean Schissel Norman, Meredith Ladik Drummond
Contributing Designer: Stacey Willey
Contributing Copyeditor and Proofreader:
Elizabeth Sedrel, Nancy Dietz
Contributing Photographers: Edmund Barr, Gordon Beall, Ed Golich, Richard Leo Johnson, Beth Singer
Contributing Illustrators: Christopher Glowacki, Ann Weiss
Cover Photographer: John Bessler
Contributing Photo Researcher: Cathy Long

SPECIAL INTEREST MEDIA
Editorial Director: Gregory H. Kayko
Content Core Director, Home: Jill Waage
Deputy Content Core Director, Home: Karman Hotchkiss
Managing Editor: Doug Kouma
Art Director: Gene Rauch
Group Editor: Lacey Howard
Copy Chief: Jennifer Speer Ramundt
Business Director: Janice Croat
Executive Editor, Books: Larry Erickson
Imaging Center Operators: Randy Manning, Michael Sturtz

MEREDITH NATIONAL MEDIA GROUP
President: Tom Harty
Executive Vice President: Doug Olson

MEREDITH CORPORATION
President and Chief Executive Officer: Stephen M. Lacy

JOHN WILEY AND SONS, INC.
Vice President and Publisher: Cindy Kitchel
Acquisitions Editor: Pam Mourourzis
Senior Production Manager: Marcia Samuels
Senior Production Editor: Lisa Burstiner

Let's decorate!

The path to a comfortable, inviting, and well-organized home begins here.

Whatever your experience, each new decorating challenge is exhilarating. But it's easy to be overwhelmed by choices and short on guidance.

That's why we've written this book. We've gathered the best ideas, advice, and inspiration to help you create a home that's beautiful and suits your family perfectly. You can explore style, learn how to use color, hang artwork, and arrange furniture—and find projects to enhance every room.

In the first section, Room Views, you'll find the most inspiring ideas for every room in the house. Then in House Tours you'll learn how a cohesive design plan creates great style for any home.

When you're ready to create a plan, turn to Workroom, the final section of this book. It's filled with the detailed information you need to make the best choices in furniture, lighting, and more.

Throughout the book we've packed the pages with our editors' best tips on color, storage, and design, plus expert advice on how to be smart with the space you have.

So whether you're refreshing a single space or redoing the whole house, we've put everything you need in these pages.

Gayle

Gayle Goodson Butler,
Editor in Chief

Top tools for your tote

Journal to sketch ideas and jot down sizes and product numbers.

Fine-point pen that won't bleed or smear.

Tape measure that's lightweight and small.

Small scissors to snip fabric and trim samples.

Multitool pocket knife with a flat-head screwdriver to open paint cans.

Digital camera or device to capture a favorite chair or pillow.

Plastic sandwich bags for swatches and receipts.

Home decorating apps such as a carpenter's level or a paint color matcher.

Clear project file to easily view project plans and samples.

Adhesive lint roller to remove fabric swatch threads.

contents

room views

Discover ideas to help redo every room in your house, and learn how to create stylish, welcoming, and adaptable spaces perfect for your family.

living rooms

The living room is the first room guests see and the perfect opportunity to showcase your style. Learn how to create a retreat for a well-lived life at home.

10 Design Basics

1. SELECT FOCUS. Create a view with a window, a fireplace, bookshelves, or an art wall. **2. DIRECT TRAFFIC.** A sofa back facing the doorway stops traffic, while a strategically placed chair directs the flow. Orient furniture to the view. **3. GO MOODY.** Dressy versus casual, or colorful versus neutral? If you're unsure of the mood, collect pictures to help define your style. Be adventurous as you create the room's look. **4. SAMPLE FIRST** by selecting fabric or wallpaper, then paint. Check paint and fabric samples in daylight and lamplight before buying. **5. SHOP SMART.** A longer sofa provides more seating in less space than several chairs. Cabinets with doors offer hideaway storage. An upholstered ottoman can serve as a coffee table and footstool. **6. GO NEUTRAL.** A neutral sofa and flooring will last through several color changes. Add bold, changeable color with less expensive accessories or wall paint. **7. CHOOSE LIGHT.** Buy for mood and utility. Consider a reading lamp, lighting over a game table, and ambient lighting to add a soft glow. **8. SIZE RUGS.** Choose a rug that's large enough for all the furniture to fit, or small enough so the rug edges just touch the furniture legs. **9. MAKE UPKEEP EASY** with washable slipcovers, scrubbable painted surfaces, and fuss-free window treatments. **10. EDIT, EDIT, EDIT.** Sort your possessions down to a chosen few.

styles we love

It's all about you. Think about your style as you study these rooms. Which elements deliver the look you want? Which inspire a new look?

COLOR AT PLAY

above left **Colors** as fresh as summer flowers set the mood in this cottage-meets-fashionista living room. The all-white background eliminates competition for the design spotlight, while a mirrored coffee table and Moorish side table shake up the classic cottage sofa and chairs.

PLAYFUL CHIC

above right **Surprise** elements, such as a shower curtain turned into wall art above the sofa, a collection of pillows stitched from vintage fabrics, and a metallic-painted coffee table, inject fun into design. Pale backgrounds make it easy to switch flea market finds whenever the mood strikes.

NATURE-INSPIRED

opposite left **Nature's** influence can be subtle: seagrass for rugs, flaxseed linen for upholstery on the French chairs, and woven baskets that hold toys. And it can be dramatic: twig art for the walls, framed butterfly specimens, and curtains the color of sunshine. A window-wrapped room? Perfection.

URBAN MODERN

opposite right **Gutsy** and strong, this cityscape style contrasts high-energy red with neutral black, gray, and stone. Streamlined furniture with exposed legs and tight upholstery provides the background for geometric patterns. Industrial touches in accessories create city-smart impact.

Making arrangements

There's an art to creating seating areas that encourage long conversations and soul-restoring lounging. Prioritize seating elements: Consider comfortable seating, pillows to adjust seat depth, ottomans for propping feet, tables for resting a beverage or a book, and adjustable lighting that can be low for conversation and bright for reading. In general, the most flexible plan includes a sofa flanked by a pair of chairs. Orient the furniture to the view, whether it's the garden outside or a wall-mounted television. Make sure each seating space is within easy reach of an occasional table and a light source. Several small, movable tables as well as floor lamps might be the best choices to achieve this goal.

styles we love

EUROPEAN REDUX
It helps to create this
style if you start with
fluted moldings and pine
floors, but the elements
work anywhere. The style
is based on the enduring
charm of vintage pieces.
Consider these: French-
and Swedish-style
furnishings, vintage
collections, and worn and
painted wood furniture.

GLOBAL COTTAGE

above left Small-space living doesn't have to be boring. Bold animal prints and exotic Asian tables add design punch to this basic room. The warm khaki walls and rug create a soothing backdrop for color and pattern. Minimal window treatments maintain an unfussy look.

TAILORED CLASSIC

above right To achieve this look, start with furniture in simple shapes executed in dark woods for drama and neutral fabrics for flexibility; add accessories that tell a story about you, including favorite colors and shapes. In a small space, include double-duty pieces such as ottomans to use as seats or tables.

What's in your living room?

If you're inspired to create a new look for your living room, it's time to take an educated look at your space and furnishings. Refresh. Consider whether any pieces can be repurposed with paint or fabric. Remove items you no longer want in the room; sell or donate them. Take snapshots of the items you love and want to keep. Stay focused. Gather your collection of tearsheets, snapshots, fabric and paint samples, and product photos. Attach them to a large piece of poster board that you can keep in the room for a few weeks. Understand light. Check out the room throughout the day to see how the changing light affects your choices. This process can take time, but it's the best way to start a living room makeover.

1 wall 2 ways

Think of an art wall as an expression of your design personality.
Gather the pieces you love, then play with the arrangement.

GO FOR BALANCE
A stack of framed silhouettes on one side of the sofa and hanging lights on the other create balance that feels comfortable and casual. The trick is to let the art pieces dominate in color and weight. Experiment with extending the collection beyond the sofa's edge.

Try this!
Cut paper shapes of framed pieces and arrange the paper on your wall before you pound a single nail.

EXPLORE THE "GALAXY" TECHNIQUE

Start with a central dominant framed piece, such as the peony silhouette. Surround it with smaller pieces in a variety of shapes, sizes, and formats. To make the arrangement hang together visually, use artwork in similar colors and themes. Balance the wall with a darker and larger piece on the bottom and a smaller piece to "crown" the top.

color palette

The secret to a vibrant color mix: choosing hues of equal intensity so no one color jumps out—and every element blends beautifully.

COLOR PALETTE
Wallpaper inspired this room's scheme of gold, green, and blue with touches of peachy pink. Find your perfect palette by pulling colors from the fabrics and artworks you love.

Bold yellow
Brighten a north-facing room with bold color. Windows and a wallpapered nook balance the yellow walls.

Mossy green
Green plays a supporting role on the coffee table and in the wallpaper's background.

Bright aqua
Aqua, a complement of yellow, adds energy. Introduce pops of this happy hue in accessories.

Try this! Create a ribbon sling for a frameless mirror. Hang mirror. Loop ribbon around the mirror; tack ribbon in place.

Color mastery

Once you've chosen a palette, here's how to apply color to a room.

Put color in its place. Gold walls and the green-painted coffee table anchor the color scheme. Blues add soothing accents.

Don't forget the floor. Like the walls, the floor has power to introduce color and warmth. The airy blue of the rug picks up wallpaper hues.

Keep color under control. Curtains closely match the walls, but the subtle ironwork pattern sets them apart without making the room look busy.

Punch up the color quotient. Pillows in pink, green, blue, and gray graphic designs add variety. Each pillow showcases a single color with white, so they complement rather than distract from the room's multicolor palette.

Add instant color. Throws tossed over the backs of the chair and sofa are easy accents to add or subtract.

pattern palette

A little pattern can be fairly easy to incorporate into a home—toss in a few pillows or a painting. Using a lot of pattern requires a sure eye. Here's how this room makes it work.

Bold botanicals
An overscale print in lime green adds drama and calls attention to the windows.

Modern lines
A geometric of wavy lines introduces a modern edge that demands attention without dominating.

Contrast leaves
Pattern and contrasting colors create a look-at-me ottoman that occupies the center of the space.

PATTERN PALETTE
To build a scheme around patterns, vary their sizes and colors. Note how the vase's bold, colorful pattern balances the curtain's oversize but paler leaves.

Pattern mastery
Learn how to create a pattern-happy house using these tips.

Pick patterns you love. Pull swatches you like and begin building a swatchbook of pattern.

Build a color scheme. Select a dominant hue, a secondary color, and an accent from the pattern. Choose tones that are slightly different to create interest.

Consider the room size. Small patterns can disappear in a large room, while big patterns can overwhelm a small space.

Focus on the pattern repeat. A large-scale print can be too big for a pillow. A complicated pattern might disappear in the folds of drapery.

Create a focal point. Patterned curtains naturally call attention to windows, while a bold geometric on a single wall can create architectural interest.

Use color repetition. It's a sure way to tie together patterns as varied as large-scale leaves and soft lines.

before & after

Think of a boxy room as a blank canvas. You can add architecture with built-ins, wainscoting, and molding, and introduce decorating flair with great furniture. Plus, you decide the best way to use the space to meet your family's needs.

BEFORE
3 common flaws

1 Architectural detail is lacking. Blank walls, no trim, popcorn ceilings.

2 Open room serves different functions. Separate or treat as one?

3 An L-shape living and dining room makes furniture-arranging a big challenge.

3 fabulous fixes

1 Add character with built-ins, molding, and paneling.

2 Unite the space by repeating architectural elements and colors.

3 Create zones using area rugs to anchor furniture groupings.

STORAGE STYLE

opposite **Built-in cabinets around the windows add a focal point to the dining end of the L-shape space. Pairing 12-inch-deep upper cabinets with deeper lower cabinets leaves a serving ledge and storage for dining gear.**

SEAT YOURSELF

below left and far right **The space under the windows offers room for seating and a big drawer for storage. It's a perfect perch for color and pattern.**

COUNT ON DETAILS

right **Architectural details using stock molding take the boring out of a boxy room. This ledge provides display space around the room at eye level.**

TAMING THE L

below right **Use a savvy furniture layout and rugs to neatly divide an L-shape space into living, dining, and office areas. It's OK to place furniture in the middle of a room, but opt for a pair of chairs rather than a sofa to keep the visual footprint light.**

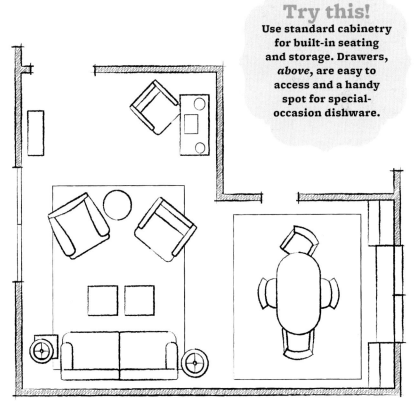

Try this!
Use standard cabinetry for built-in seating and storage. Drawers, *above*, are easy to access and a handy spot for special-occasion dishware.

2-stage makeover

Ready to redo? Our two-step method starts with rearranging the furniture and sets a plan that gets better as you add new pieces.

start with the basics

1 "Float" furniture to create better flow.

2 Define the furniture grouping with a rug.

3 Place tables where they're handy.

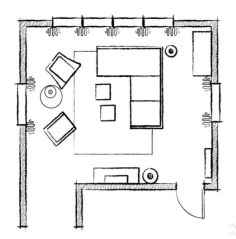

replace and add

1 Rearrange the furniture for more seating.

2 Use bunching tables as flexible coffee tables.

3 Add shelves for storage and display.

PERFECTING THE PLAN

The key to a successful furniture plan is to have stage two in mind at the beginning. Gradually purchase new pieces. This strategy buys time for your budget to keep up with the makeover.

style made simple | curtains

Think day and night when deciding how to dress windows. You'll want sun control during the day and privacy after dark.

CAFÉ CURTAIN

above left **Consider choosing a half curtain for a short window. This pair tops a window seat and coordinates with other curtains in the room. Adding a curtain using clip rings is an easy-up solution. Opt for wood rings and rod to complement the pine woodwork.**

CLIP-TOP PANELS + BLIND

above right **Clip-on rings on the top and a panel that puddles on the floor offer the ultimate in flexibility. It's truly a one-size-fits-all option. Add a bamboo blind for light control. You may need to line the shade for nighttime privacy, or simply close the panels.**

DOORWAY PANEL

opposite left **Curtain panels work wonders between rooms as well. They divide spaces without closing them off and offer splashes of color and pattern. Look for specialty swing-arm curtain rods that suspend the rod from a vertical surface at only one end.**

GROMMET PANELS + ROLLER SHADE

opposite right **This tailored window combination gets an extra dose of style with grommets on the curtain tops and a roller shade covered with fabric. Purchase a roller shade kit at a fabrics store so you can use your favorite fabric.**

Problem-solving window treatments

Use window treatments to visually narrow windows, raise ceilings, and balance placement. Here are a few ideas. Widen a narrow window by surrounding it with curtains that hang outside the frame. Raise a too-low ceiling visually by hanging curtain panels from the ceiling or installing a top shade near the ceiling. Revamp an awkwardly positioned window (one that's too high or too low on the wall) by hanging a curtain from the center of the window to the floor or topping it with a valance that hides the window top. Minimize differences by treating windows of similar but varying sizes all the same. Add style pizzazz with a bold fabric. Test it out by hanging a yard of fabric from a curtain rod. Preserve the architectural impact of windows by tucking shades inside the frames.

style made simple | mantels

Make the most of your mantel and its prime decorating real estate with these four winning suggestions that deliver top billing.

Try this!
Add decals to the inside of a vinyl lampshade for an easy-on-easy-off makeover.

ELEGANT SCRIPT

opposite **Installing a chic monogram decal above a fireplace creates a focal point and solves the whole wall art issue. The peel-and-stick decal is easy to apply. Finish off the arrangement with a grouping of interesting vases.**

NATURAL BALANCE

top right **Symmetry starts here with a centered piece of driftwood. Add pairs: candles, pots filled with natural objects, and hanging prints. It's OK to use natural objects that look similar without exactly matching. Symmetrical doesn't have to mean stiff.**

SMART REPETITION

middle right **It's a basic rule of design: Multiples, such as this series of framed maps, have more impact than singles. Make sure to use frames that are at least one-third the height of the chimney breast.**

COLOR UNITY

bottom right **Go off the grid with asymmetry, but keep the arrangement cohesive with a unified color palette. Balance a tall, large object with several smaller ones. Nestle the assemblage tightly together to increase its visual weight, and overlap shapes to create layers.**

29

Try this!
Add interest
by gathering a
collection on top of
a tall cabinet.

Try these ideas for incorporating books—a few or a library full—into the living room.

FOR THE COLLECTOR
opposite **Turn a glass-front cabinet into dust-free display for a collection of books and decorative dishware.**

FOR THE BUDGET
top left **Standard steel office shelves—extra tall and slim at 13 ½ inches deep—contain a library.**

FOR BOOKWORMS
top right **Stack current reading material on a mantel where favorite tomes tout your personality.**

FOR PLANT LOVERS
middle left **Stand up books in style using a planted container. Stones keep it from tipping.**

FOR DISPLAY
middle right **Hang framed prints from vertical bookcase supports to add art to a room.**

FOR THE COOK
bottom left **Tuck cookbook storage under a pair of windows for a smart use of a little space.**

FOR THE LOUNGER
bottom right **Stacking books on a coffee table elevates decorative objects. Keep one open to a favorite page for fun.**

31

dining rooms

Serve up a dining room so appetizing in its comfort, versatility, and style that your guests will linger long after the last plate has been cleared.

10 Design Basics **1. MATCH YOUR DINING TABLE SHAPE** to your room shape. Rectangles go best in rectangular rooms, squares or circles in square rooms. **2. SPLIT UP A MATCHED SET.** Mixing eras, styles, and textures of furniture keeps a look fresh. Pair a formal wood table with bamboo chairs painted a glossy red. **3. THINK CLEARANCE.** Position the table to keep pathways clear, especially the one to the kitchen. Allow 36 inches of space all around the perimeter of the table so chairs pull out without bumping walls or furniture. **4. BEST SEATS.** Slipper and side chairs snuggle up to the table, while armchairs gobble up room—so place them at table ends. Upholstered settees add a café feel. **5. BE A STAIN FIGHTER.** Choose seat cushions in stain-camouflaging patterns or spill-repelling materials, or buy removable, washable slipcovers. **6. DON'T HIDE THE CHINA.** Love your table service? Display it on open shelves or hang platters on a wall, then incorporate its motifs or colors in linens, drapes, and paint. **7. PROPORTION AND POSITION.** Choose a center light fixture that's one-third the size of the table. If it's a pendant, hang it 30 to 36 inches above the tabletop. **8. FOR BISTRO GLOW,** install sconces and dimmer switches. **9. UNDER FOOT.** Pick a rug 4 feet wider than the table on all sides so chairs slide out smoothly. **10. GO FOR SOME DRAMA.** Create a focal point: Hang a grid of eye-catching prints above a buffet; highlight a wall in graphic wallpaper; pick a stunning chandelier.

styles we love

Though dining rooms may share the basic ingredients of a table and chairs, that's where the similarities end. Here, a taste of our favorite looks.

TRANSPARENT TRUTH

above left **A modern, minimalist look works well in tight spaces. Here, a slick glass top with an airy base reduces the visual bulk. Chairs with skinny legs and bases also make the room feel spacious. Hanging wall storage keeps floors clear. Airy burlap drapes hung at ceiling level add height, filter sun, and don't close in the room. The shapely pendant lamp is a lightweight, too.**

BRIGHT ATTITUDE

above right **Give a vintage home like this energy with cheerful, saturated colors. Juice up walls with citrusy orange paint. Update the formal dining set with a bright contrasting color such as apple-green fabric. Brightening period millwork with white paint lets colors pop. Keep it casual—and connected to the garden theme—with bare-wood floors, undressed windows or French doors, and a whimsical flower-motif chandelier.**

NATURAL SELECTIONS

opposite left **Connect to nature for a laid-back yet sophisticated room. The key: layering natural textures against a clean, soft backdrop. Here, it's wicker chairs on a seagrass rug with a linen runner and terra-cotta ceramics on the table. Breezy blue walls add softness, as do downy chair pillows and an understated chandelier. Simple shades and shutters let sunlight in.**

TAKE SHAPE

opposite right **Orderly lines, symmetry, and lack of heavy ornamentation allow Colonial homes to harmonize easily with today's looks. Provide a gallery-like backdrop by painting walls and built-ins white. Then introduce strong modern shapes and metallic finishes. Here, it's curved-back chairs in a neutral fabric; an oversize, plain pendant; and a pedestal table with a shimmery base. Pare decorative objects down to one color.**

Room for a crowd

Maximize space in a squeezed dining room with flexible furniture and arranging. **Tables:** Dropleaf tables and tables with slide-in leaves, for instance, expand at a moment's notice when company calls. Circular tables—especially ones on pedestal bases—let more chairs gather around. A pair of semicircular demilune tables, console tables, or midsize square tables can stand against walls until guests arrive, then be joined to form one larger table at mealtime. **Storage:** If a sideboard or china cabinet won't fit, hang rows of open shelves to hold serving pieces. (Be sure to anchor them securely to wall studs.) **Seating:** An L-shape, built-in banquette recruits an underutilized room corner and can provide hidden storage under its seating. Replace chairs with low, backless benches or stackable stools. When not needed, they can tuck neatly under the table, along walls, or into another room or hallway.

double-duty spaces

Put valuable square footage to work all day by designing the dining room for use between meals.

LOUNGE ACT
Instead of a built-in banquette, try a plush settee. Though it's formal, this settee's generous size, cushy pillows, and friendly striped upholstery relax its look. Tall bookcases provide storage. A crystal-drop chandelier turns the sunny space into an intimate dining room after dark.

PART-TIME OFFICE

above left **If you your dining room doubles as an office, reserve space inside the buffet table or hutch to stash work files, or study materials. That way these much-needed supplies don't get in the way visually or physically when you use the room for dining. This console keeps reference media on one side, barware and china on the other. Frosted-glass doors put up a neat front.**

SHELF SERVICE

above right **In a small room that moonlights as an office, play up its cozy quotient by adding a wall of built-in bookcases for office storage. Reserve lower, closed-door cabinets for computer equipment and files; use open shelves to display reference books and decorative objects. With this much open shelving, constant editing of books and magazines into neat rows is a must! Anchor the table area with a lantern-shape center light.**

Storage strategies

The dining room is often where family members spread out projects or plop down mail. Keep it tidy and storage-savvy with the right organization. Designate a bin for whatever tends to find a temporary home on the table. This can be permanent storage or a handled tote to move things to their rightful room. **Don't feel you have to put everything** dining-related in your hutch. It's OK to split up a set of china if you're using only a few pieces. Consider long-term storage of the remainder in other rooms, such as upper cabinets in a kitchen. Keep a list tacked inside your hutch door reminding you where the overflow is stored. You'll relish the storage space it frees up in the dining room.

color palette

Moss green hues ranging from crisp bright apple to earthy olive can soothe or energize a room. Learn how and where to use this versatile color to give rooms a boost of style.

peat moss, a black-tinged green, is a color chameleon, looking elegant with cream, preppy with navy, and posh with nut brown. **Try it:** on walls.

nettle, warm and subtle, is a supporting player. **Try it:** on kitchen cabinets with oil-rubbed hardware.

sprout, with its hit of bright yellow, steers this color into brazen territory. **Try it:** on a hutch or buffet or in accessories such as vases or boxes.

lily pad, a cool, grounded neutral, calms a room. **Try it:** in a family room or home office.

lettuce leaf, with eye-opening yellow undertones, looks especially crisp in rooms with dark wood floors. **Try it:** on walls, in curtains, and as pillows.

Color mastery

Use these saturation points to create a dining room palette that's anything but garden variety.

Lay the groundwork. Shapely gray furniture and creamy walls provide a neutral canvas on which to build a color scheme. Easily added accessories in fresh greens add crisp color, pattern, and energy. Touches of white in the textiles and ceramics tie them all together.

Team players. Greens have a way of working well together—nature is a prime example. So don't worry about matching shades in fabrics, paint, and rugs. These celery drapes befriend a lime rug.

Balance of pattern. When working with textiles in similar shades, vary their patterns and sizes to avoid boredom. This broad-stripe rug, tight trellis-pattern drapes, and bold floral pillows keep eyes alert and interested.

Get your greens. When green's undertone is blue, it has a restful, quieting power—a good choice for a bedroom. With a yellow undertone, green is sassy—like in this dining room—and good for any gathering space or on a standout piece of furniture.

before & after

Take a vaulted-ceiling breakfast room from famine to visual feast with sunny colors, comfy furniture, and garden touches. A coordinated approach produces a casual but sophisticated look.

AFTER
3 fabulous fixes

1 Paint one wall for interest. Soften and equalize the windows with coverings.

2 Add a pedestal table and slipper chairs for casual comfort.

3 A large drum shade hung at the proper height holds its own.

BEFORE
3 common flaws

1 White walls are bland and the windows are mismatched.

2 A too-long table with uncomfortable side chairs is uninviting.

3 The spindly chandelier is hung way too high.

Try this!
A decorative platter is a fresh alternative to framed art.

Adding up the details
A dining room sings with style.

Paint with purpose.
A cheery blue plays up the tall wall with the arched window. Leaving the spaces between arch and lower windows and between window and the floor white gives the look of one large window.

Treat windows.
Floral panels soften the large window. Hung below the arched window, they balance the wall's height. The panels' scalloped border breaks up the whiteness. The side window, dressed in a Roman shade in the deep blue of the drapery trim, is hung at the same height, equalizing the two windows.

Curves add character.
A chunky round table and a drum-shade light soften a boxy space. The fixture is sized so diners won't bump it when leaning in (a 42-inch shade paired with a 52-inch table). Hung 3 feet above the table, the light is visually connected to the table. An oval braided rug adds more curves.

Sitting pretty.
Slipper chairs add softness. Their short slipcovers are outdoor fabrics in a sunny hue with ribbon details and piping to play up the blue wall. The wicker chairs remain; their woven texture reflects the new light's nubby raffia shade.

style made simple | organization

What's the hostess with the mostest's secret weapon? A china cabinet that's pretty and put-together with a plethora of savvy storage options.

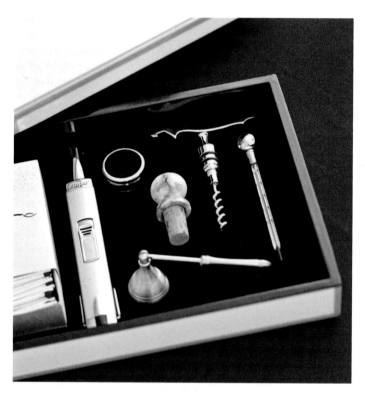

SPRING TO ACTION

left Spring-loaded dividers designed for dresser drawers handily customize any size hutch or buffet drawer. Use the dividers to create individual sections for storing neat stacks of cloth napkins and orderly rows of candles.

CREATE A BOXED SET

above left Earn the title "savvy hostess" by keeping a felt-lined box stocked with matches, corkscrews, and other entertaining necessities tucked in a drawer. With a pretty box like this, you can leave it on a buffet or side table all evening for easy access as needed.

DIVIDE AND CONQUER

above right Add a wire shelf rack to double storage space for plates and make them easier to access. (Slip coffee filters between plates to prevent nicks.) A cardboard box with dividers made to store socks keeps small tabletop items, such as napkin rings and votive candles, at the ready. A list of items stored elsewhere in the home taped to the inside of a cabinet door eliminates searching time.

Display perfection

Create a landscape of shape and color while maximizing storage on hutch shelves.

Set the scene.
Make dishes stand out by lining the back of your cabinet with decorative paper affixed with double-sided tape. Choose a color or pattern that flatters— but does not compete with—your china pattern and room style.

Think in layers.
Consider shelves a barren landscape in need of shapes and silhouettes. Lean plates against the back of a few shelves and display other items such as compotes in front to highlight their forms. Group like materials, such as crystal, for a well-ordered appearance.

Stack it up.
Make the best use of vertical space by stacking cups with their saucers. The look is sculptural and serviceable.

Be bottom heavy.
Store large items such as platters and tureens on bottom shelves for visual balance and to make them easy to carry to the table.

room elements | chandeliers

Dining rooms come to life after dark, so choose a fixture that adds style to your space and supplies the perfect glow for unhurried meals and lively conversation.

REVEALING LOOK
When lit, this mesh-encased pendant reveals a romantic drop-crystal chandelier within. Using simple lights in opposing "rugged and refined" materials is an easy way to make a house feel 21st-century fresh.

BLACK OUT

top left **Fill the air space of a vaulted-ceiling home with a center-stage fixture like this large candelabra-style chandelier.**

MIRROR IMAGES

top right **Anchor a long dining table with a trio of pendant lights. These update the look of old utility lights with modern mercury glass. Bonus: A string of pendants offers focused task lighting.**

FLIRTATIOUS LOOK

middle left **This dressy chandelier drips with crystal and opaline elements. To dress up a bare fixture, shop antiques stores for orphan drop crystal pendants and links.**

ECLECTIC CURRENT

middle right **For a surprise twist, seek a center light whose materials nod to the past with a sculptural and current form. This hoop fixture marries old iron carriage wheels and Thomas Edison's filament lights with floating-in-air form.**

ON THE BALL

bottom left **Add to an iron chandelier with swags crafted from plain wood balls in three sizes. The contrast of old and new, woodsy and modern, makes any space or accessory fresh.**

CANDLE POWER

bottom right **Reproduction light fixtures duplicate the look of candles but offer the modern convenience of electricity. This fixture recalls an 18th-century whale oil light.**

45

style made simple | storage

Simple open white bookcases are a wonderful storage-and-service solution for almost any dining room. Choose wide or narrow, shallow or deep—then use the pieces horizontally or vertically.

HAPPY HOUR
To create this store-and-serve buffet, hang a pair of narrow, shallow bookcases horizontally, then slip a third on the floor below. Install the middle bookcase at countertop height—36 inches is typical—so it can moonlight as a swanky bar or cake-serving station. Stock one unit with woven totes to hold table linens. Use weight-appropriate wall anchors to hang the bookcases.

OPEN WIDE

More slender than a china hutch, a wide and deep bookcase in a size-compromised dining area eats up less floor space, provides miles of storage, and offers an open canvas for pretty displays. Push a backless bookcase against a wallpapered or richly painted wall, as seen here, and you've created an artful visual effect.

entries

Have them at "hello": Create an entryway that welcomes family and friends with its warm, charming style and smart storage ideas.

10 Design Basics

1. GREET VISITORS WARMLY. Brighten an entry with cheerful wallpaper or a sunny paint color, a patterned runner, and a gallery of favorite prints or family portraits. **2. USE OPTICAL TRICKS.** Raise a ceiling visually: Furnish your foyer with tall furniture (a slim secretary or coat lockers, for instance) or hang striped wallpaper to guide eyes upward. Lower too-tall ceilings by creating focus at ground level. Add an eye-catching rug or install a chair-rail a third of the way up from the floor (usually at 32 to 36 inches). **3. FAKE A FOYER.** In a house without a foyer, a console table, mirror, and coat rack beside the front door say "center hall" without the walls. **4. THINK OUTSIDE THE BOX.** Reassign a slim dresser, secretary, or bookcase to an entry; use the drawers and shelves for storage. **5. SHELF-SERVE.** In a foyer too narrow for a table, hang a slim shelf instead. **6. USE OVERHEAD SPACE** to hang cabinets and cubbies high on the wall. **7. DESIGNATED DIVIDERS.** Outfit a back entry with freestanding closet components such as coat lockers and shoe cubbies, one per family member. **8. LIGHT FANTASTIC.** Plug-in sconces and table lamps add soft, welcoming light—no electrician needed. **9. CONCEAL CLUTTER** using lidded boxes in coordinating shapes and styles. They maintain an orderly appearance and hide not-so-pretty but necessary items. **10. LOADING DOCK.** Recharge electronics in a plug-in station so they're easy to grab on the way out.

styles we love

Back- and side-door entries wear many hats, from coatroom to storeroom, so outfit yours with handsome style and hardworking organization.

IT'S A WASH
above left **Check muddy paws and boots at the back door with an in-floor sink, walls, and shower seat made from waterproof surfaces. A handheld shower installed low to the ground handily hoses off dirt. The fold-down bench acts as a drying rack for wet swimsuits or mittens. For a casual country look, the area is tailored with baskets, beaded-board walls, and rugged plank floors.**

FOR FEET AND PAWS
above right **Above-ground shoe cubbies make room for a dog den in this open closet. It's designed around what the homeowners owned—an antique cupboard, big baskets, Fido, and footwear. Classic tailoring comes from white cabinetry and millwork to contrast with the dark floor. To withstand water, grime, and paws, the owners chose slate tile; resilient sheet flooring is also a solid, affordable choice.**

PREFERRED SEATING
opposite left **A bench seat crafted from a pair of cabinet drawers becomes a smart place to tuck seasonal items such as hats and mittens. A homespun cushion makes for a soft landing. Continue the "uptown country" look with an iron scrollwork chandelier, a cleaning closet disguised as an antique hutch, beaded paneling, crown molding, and a black-painted French door.**

THRIFTY TRICKS
opposite right **This mudroom relies on ready-to-assemble storage modules from a home center: two base drawers, locker-style cabinets, and a partial wall. Stock baseboard and crown molding seamlessly integrate cabinets and walls. Wipe-on color washes give assorted baskets personality and visual continuity. A vivid orange cushion and bird-silhouette pillow add a dose of sophisticated decoration and comfort.**

Dry ideas

Rain happens. And, depending on where you live, so does snow. Prepare your entry for wet weather with these handy additions. Place wire cooling racks on top of large cookie baking sheets or serving trays to keep wet, muddy boots and shoes from dirtying floors. Nail a lineup of large bulldog clips to the wall or a cabinet for hanging wet gloves and snowy knit caps to dry. Use an umbrella stand, wastebasket, tall cylinder vase, or garden urn to stash drippy umbrellas as soon as they come in the door. Have a place to sit, such as a bench, chest, or stool, for pulling off slushy boots or wet shoes. Stock the bench or a basket with a stack of towels for drying off. Consider an indoor-outdoor rug for its durability and dirty-catching function. Plus, many can be hosed off for easy cleaning.

small spaces

Even a sliver of space at the front door can live large when it's tuned up with smart function and good looks.

THE HIGHER-UPS

above left **Positioning a simple shelf and sturdy coat hooks high on a wall frees up floor space, making a crowded entry feel more spacious. The vertical striping of beaded board enhances the clean, streamlined look. A gang of baskets stashes not-so-pretty items out of sight.**

FRESH COAT

above right **Reboot a vintage coat tree in a bright coat of paint that shouts "welcome." Turquoise, grass green, and bright yellow are vivid hues popular today to revive and play up the shapes of classic furniture pieces.**

LETTER PERFECT

opposite left **May we have a word or two with your boring foyer? Press-on decals in a varied-typeface alphabet put the "fun" in function when installed above coat hooks. For error-proof place-markers, install hooks beneath the first letters of your children's names. If you tire of the decal, peel it off; most decals are gentle to walls.**

UNDER SERVED

opposite right **Don't overlook the potential of the slimmest of wall spaces. Tucked under an awning window, a "coat locker" built with 1×6s, crown molding, beaded-board paneling, and row of hooks adds ample organization and a classic architectural detail.**

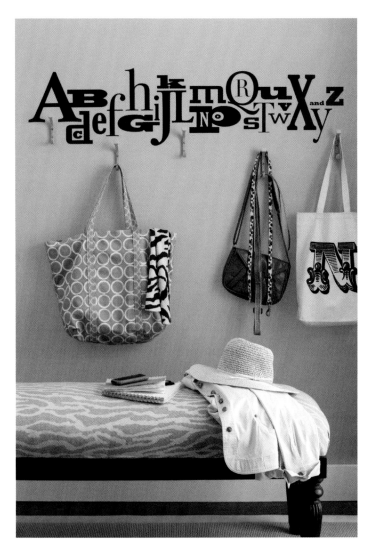

What to stash where you dash

When you're rushing out the door, taking the time to search for life's little necessities can cause quite a speed bump in your schedule. Keep your entry stocked with these items: change for parking meters, lint remover, small flashlight, bandages, pens and pencils, sticky notes, safety pins, mini sewing repair kit, hair elastics or headbands, lip balm, sunscreen, bug spray, postage stamps, and an extra set of car keys. Organize them in baskets and totes and on hooks and shelves specially designated for these on-the-go items.

color palette

Hello, yellow! Let's give a warm welcome to yellow in a mellow shade that's uplifting yet solidly down to earth.

bee pollen, a dusky rather than bright shade. **Try it:** painted on a bench, occasional chair, or console table.

cornmeal, sweet but with a little bite. **Try it:** on the walls of a foyer or powder room.

butter, a pale, universally pleasing yellow. **Try it:** on the walls of any room.

lemon drop, a yummy shade that makes a friendly statement. **Try it:** in an entry, on a dresser, on a lamp base, or for a group of frames.

soft dijon, a ruddy gold that looks sharp. **Try it:** on an accent wall behind a black bookcase.

Color mastery

Yellow visually expands a room, making it well suited for hallways and entries. Here, warm thoughts on choosing the right yellow.

Avoid overwhelming a space. Shop for dusky yellows grounded by a dose of brown—Dijon mustard, beeswax, or cornsilk, for example.

Baby steps. Warm up to yellow by using it on a single, eye-catching surface: Coat a bench in muted bee pollen, paint an accent wall mustard, or line the back of a cupboard in a ruddy gold wallpaper.

Unlikely duos. Burnt yellows are traditionally paired with blue, but try them with dove gray or deep aubergine for an unexpectedly sophisticated combo. Other options for browned-down yellows are fresh green and periwinkle.

Play it safe. When painting an entire room yellow, start soft with a pale cornmeal or cornsilk. For more drama, paint one wall a more intense version of the same yellow (look two or more places down on the paint chip for a good companion).

UPBEAT BUT NOT BLINDING, this entry's cornmeal-color wallpaper is warm and welcoming. Pops of blue, the traditional best buddy of yellow, appears in a lamp and wall-hung plates. Brown stripes in the rug and dark bronze dresser hardware complement the wallpaper's subtle brown undertone.

before & after

A front hallway is more than a way to get from point A to B. End "tunnel vision" and see a space filled with warmth and personality as well as function.

3 common flaws

1 Barren walls, dull floors, and a worn bench are a style dead end.

2 Storage for a family's coats, backpacks, and shoes is nonexistent.

3 A ho-hum staircase that's a downer blends into the hallway.

3 fabulous fixes

1 Painted and primped, this entry puts its best foot forward.

2 A new bench opens for ample hidden storage.

3 A classic-stripe staircase runner is uplifting.

STOP-AND-GO SPACE

opposite **A bench with storage under the seat provides a home for sports equipment, blankets, and seasonal gear. Pillows and a cushion make the bench cozier. An architectural salvage piece adds history to a new home and draws the eye back through the hall. A mirror is a handy last-check grooming spot. A café table holds a tin planter for mail, and saucers stash keys and change.**

DURABLE GOODS

above left **To counter the wear and tear on an entry and stairway, use indoor-outdoor polypropylene rugs—they're stain-resistant and bleachable. Stripes and tight patterns hide dirt. Sturdy baskets, one for each family member, slip out of sight under the bench. Kids can drop items when they first enter the home and find hats and mittens when it's time to leave.**

ESCALATING STYLE

above right **Treat the stairs as part of the hall "room" by coordinating color and style. Here, a set of simply matted and framed lacy handkerchiefs contributes elegant color and shape in the cottage style of the space. Function is still paramount: Shoes that used to pile up have an orderly home on an antiqued copper-finish boot tray.**

Try this!
Paint bold diagonal lines up a staircase wall for a no-nails-needed wainscoting.

style made simple | slim tables

A narrow table is all you need to turn an entry into a destination. Add a light source and artwork, and you've got a winning formula.

CASUAL GALLERY

above left **Use a skinny sofa table with traditional lines as a pretty platform for art and accessories that change with the season. Anchor the table with a large mirror to bounce light. Lean framed seasonal images gently against the mirror for easy replacement. Change the throw rug each season—here, it's an inexpensive jute runner in a bold floral pattern.**

KEEP A LOW PROFILE

above right **A simple Parsons table takes a turn as a foyer drop zone. Its simple lines make it a sure fit in modern spaces. There's plenty of room underneath for footwear and a hamper to hold baseball gloves, leashes, and more. On top there's room for a lamp, wallets and purses, and a recharging station. For art above the table, bigger is almost always better. Just keep it within the boundaries of the table below.**

THROW A CURVE

opposite left **A table that's at least 30 inches tall and no more than 18 inches deep leaves room for traffic in an entry. A curved, or demilune, table is good for tight spaces because there are no hard corners to bump. Hang photos in a grid for a gallery effect. Repurpose a tray from the kitchen to contain keys and change. No coat closet? Pull in a sturdy, wide-legged coatrack.**

MAKE IT PERSONAL

opposite right **As guests pass through your foyer, offer them a glimpse of your personality. This antique English turned-leg table provides a perch for eclectic accessories such as Asian ceramics and an African carved-wood box. The table's open, splay-legged form is practical, allowing a large basket to tuck beneath for storing newspaper, firewood, blankets, or whatever item needs a home.**

Dirty jobs

Entry floors are the opportunity to catch all the flotsam and jetsam attached to feet (and paws) as they step in from the outdoors. Hard surfaces such as tile or well-sealed wood are good base layers, but to stop dirt from being tracked through the house, choose a hardworking rug. Generously sized throw rugs in washable materials can be as pretty as they are practical. Natural-fiber rugs including jute and sisal have toothy surfaces to grab and hold dirt that can later be vacuumed up. A runner made of carpet tiles is another sturdy option. Because all of these choices are free-floating, you can quickly and inexpensively refresh the look of your entry each season.

get organized | entry closet

Transform a cramped and cluttered entry closet into a pretty catchall space for a busy family.

Try this!
Wrap your closet's back wall in wallpaper.

OPEN TO POSSIBILITY To manage a family's storage needs, a coat closet was custom built with tall locker-like compartments on top (measure your coats to determine how tall to make the lockers) and cubbies on the bottom. The cubbies are tall and deep enough to double as a bench. Adjustable shelving fits baskets and boot trays. For easy access to the storage, the doors and surrounding walls that framed the closet were removed prior to building the lockers.

GET HOOKED

top left **Put your closet's barren back wall to good use. Nail pretty hooks to 1×4s to get the look of an old coatrack.**

BASKET CASE

top right **Choose baskets as pretty alternatives to plastic bins. Boost the style by labeling each basket with old typesetting numbers or letters. Since these appear backwards, use only a couple on each basket to ensure they're easily read.**

NEW ROLES

middle left **Repurpose vintage finds as interesting clutter catchers. An old wood box, for instance, stores postcards and letters.**

GET THE MESSAGE

middle right **Turn an unused side wall into a communications center. Install simple molding as a ledge for holding pens and paper receipts; use cup hooks for keys and leashes; and coat the wall with magnetic and whiteboard paints for a message board.**

PAN HANDLED

bottom left **Shop for oversize baking sheets at restaurant-supply shops and use them to contain the dirt and slush of shoes. Add felt pads on the bottom to avoid scratching floors.**

DRESS UP

bottom right **Dress old or reproduction swim locker baskets with striped tea toweling. This trick also hides clutter.**

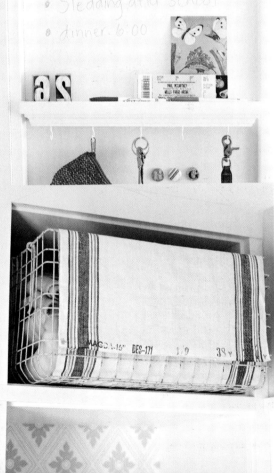

family rooms

Put family and living together, and there's sure to be wear and tear. Here's how to design a space that's up to the challenge and still looks good.

10 Design Basics

1. STAIN PROOF. Opt for fibers treated for soil- and stain-resistance, including indoor/outdoor rugs and fabrics. **2. ZONE FOR USE** by splitting a large family room using furniture: a table and chairs for games at one end and a sectional for TV watching at the other. **3. STASH AWAY.** Reduce clutter by providing a place for everything with baskets, bins, and drawers. **4. KEEP THE PEACE.** Direct traffic around and behind TV viewers. Place a game table and chairs where conversations won't drown out the TV. **5. FOCUS ON MEDIA.** Make the room work for its primary activity by orienting furniture to the screen. If the room has a fireplace, place the television on the same wall. **6. SPREAD SOFTNESS.** Sink-in seating, soft flooring, and fabric at the windows keep the room comfortable. **7. REPEAT THYSELF.** Unify a space by repeating colors, materials, and patterns. A pattern can be used just once, but always incorporate a color at least three times. **8. GET THE LIGHT RIGHT** by planning for all uses. Allow for bright lighting for a project and soft background lighting for watching movies. Attach lamps to cords with dimmers. **9. COMPUTE.** Set up easy access for using computers: a coffee table or ottoman large enough to hold supplies when working on a laptop, or a dedicated desk area for two or more computers. **10. BUILD IN** bookcases and cabinets to hold everything from a flat-screen TV to gaming consoles. For a tidy look, use a cabinet with doors to hide the gear.

styles we love

It's all about living, of course, but there's real heart in a space that begins with making room for everyone in the family.

PURE COTTAGE
above left **Snug and comfortable, cottage style is perfect for a raised-to-the-rafters family room. Beaded-board ceilings and board-and-batten walls add texture. Built-ins make a place for everything. Patterned fabrics offer spill-camouflaging covers for chairs and sofas.**

COLOR PLAY
above right **Bright colors and lively fabrics make a basement family room feel sunnier. Save the brightest pops of color for accessories that are easy to exchange for fashion's latest hues. Symmetrical shelves outfitted with baskets tame the media mess and create a focal point wall.**

GLOBAL REDUX
opposite **Vacation souvenirs gathered around the globe add design punch. Settle them in with neutral walls and furnishings accented with pops of high-energy red. Use black (in the stove, windows, art frames, and furniture) for definition.**

Try this!
Create an instant "slipcover" with a row of pillows.

Ready to go green?

Do it wisely, and the budget for your family room project will stay in the black while the style factor rises. Go big. Make the most eco-conscious choices on the big stuff—floors, walls, furniture. Spruce up furniture you already own, built-ins, and walls with paint—containing zero VOCs (volatile organic compounds), of course. "Re" think. Resell or donate what won't work. Reupholster or slipcover sofas and chairs. If buying new, choose frames made from certified-sustainable wood and recycled metal springs. Look for cushions made from renewable resources such as soy and corn rather than the standard petroleum-base foams. Step lightly. Opt for reclaimed wood flooring or less expensive certified flooring harvested in an Earth-friendly way. Buy carpeting made from renewable resources such as corn sugars or recycled plastic.

REFINED RUSTIC
Wood-paneled walls provide a surprising background for tufted chairs and an ottoman. The effect is comfortable, relaxing, and family friendly. Neutrals keep the scheme flexible, while accessories keep it interesting. Note how a rug stretches from end to end for warmth and ease.

Try this! Elevate objects to star status by repeating them across a mantel.

BUNGALOW MODERN
above left **Modern art and wing chairs with contemporary silhouettes contrast with classic architecture in this good-enough-for-company space. Exercise color fun by choosing chairs and more in bold hues. Play a surprising matchmaker by pairing fine art and paper lanterns or gourds and fine china.**

UPDATED COTTAGE
above right **Update a family room by pairing classic pieces, such as a tufted and nailhead-trimmed ottoman, with streamlined modern shapes, such as the sectional. Play solid fabrics in soft tones against the bold graphic patterns used on pillows. Coordinate the color palette from kitchen to family room to make the space cohesive.**

Divide to conquer

A family room or great-room is often large. Break it into activity areas to increase versatility. Focus Points A table and chairs at one end can be used for games. Use a corner out of the traffic for a computer station where parents can monitor usage. Relaxation Zone A sectional at one end can gather family and friends around the fireplace or television. A separate area with lamps and a small table accommodates readers. Flex Factor Make the multiuse space work for everyone with smart choices: Furniture with casters makes rearranging easy and fun and right-size storage keeps clutter off-limits.

color palette

Spice tones naturally season rooms with warmth and character. Create interest by varying the tones from dark cinnamon to golden mustard.

deep saffron, a rich gold with brown undertones complements wood floors and furniture. **Try it:** on a focal point wall or wainscoting.

golden ginger, creamy and almost neutral, warms up walls. **Try it:** to add a warm note to ceilings in a family room.

smoky paprika, a bold color best used sparingly, adds heat to a design scheme. **Try it:** as an accent color inside a bookcase, for lamp bases, or in a rug.

sweet cinnamon, a rich and dark hue, can be used as an accent to ground the other spice tones. **Try it:** as a painted finish for cabinetry or a game table.

dry mustard, with its yellow-citron tones, acts as a rich neutral perfect for backdrops. **Try it:** as the background color for rugs, curtains, or pillows.

Color mastery

Here's how to add a little spice to your life at any time of year.

Balance neutrals. Spicy hues that are intensely saturated even out earthy grays and browns. Add a richly colored throw or pillow to energize a neutral scheme.

Combine warm and cool. For an interesting twist, pair warm and cool hues, such as a muted chili pepper and cream pattern with pale celadon walls. A cool contrasting color freshens the warm palette.

Add a dash of spice. Use the boldest of these colors as accents: contrasting trim on neutral curtains, a colorful throw on a neutral sofa, or a vase of russet mums on a wood coffee table.

Serve up. Spice hues are ideal for kitchens and dining rooms because they stimulate appetite and conversation. Use them for china, linens, and centerpieces.

Try this! Create a custom rug using carpet tiles.

before & after

Flexible space is key to family living. Here it includes a homework zone that clears out for entertaining, a U-shape seating area for quiet talks around the fire or for watching football games on TV, and a reading zone for one.

3 fabulous fixes

1 Update furnishings with bold patterns and bright colors.

2 "Float" furniture so it's usable from both sides of the room.

3 Create a homework zone that parents can monitor.

BEFORE
3 common flaws

1 Dated, slouchy decor doesn't suit the needs of an active family.

2 Space is poorly used with the furniture lined up along the walls.

3 Set up for a single use, the room has no place for homework.

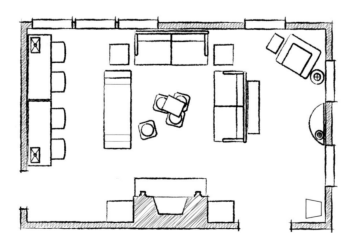

Try this!
Use four movable
tables instead
of one big
coffee table.

before & after

A can of paint, a little muscle to move furniture, and a "shopping" trip around your home can yield a fresh and inspiring makeover. Start by coating walls with a light-reflecting hue. Pull the furniture forward to the edge of the rug to create a cozy seating area.

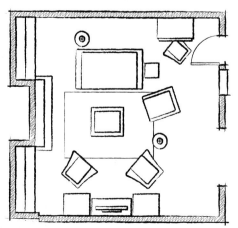

BEFORE

3 common flaws

1 The dark wall color soaks up light.

2 Bulky furniture is crowded into too little space.

3 The fireplace wall, usually a room's focal point, lacks focus.

3 fabulous fixes

1 Brighten the room with pale yellow walls.

2 Remove heavy furniture and replace with lightweight wicker chairs for an airy look.

3 Organize and draw focus to the bookcases with baskets and art.

Try this!
Top an ottoman with a tray for an instant coffee table.

style made simple | 1 coffee table 3 ways

Spin an unfinished coffee table into a surface that sings. Try one of these three fun variations.

NEAT AND SWEET

opposite **A skirt in a pretty floral gives the basic coffee table a vintage vibe and conceals anything stashed on the shelf. Use hook-and-loop tape to attach the skirt to the table base. Create a distressed look with paint in two tones to boost the flea market appeal. Top with a lace runner to complete the illusion.**

SLEEK AND CHIC

above left **Play up the coffee table's contemporary lines with contrasting colors and edgy materials. Shorten the legs and add casters to make the table mobile. Dark stain adds drama; a top and drawer fronts covered with grass cloth create the contrast. Cool fabric boxes on the shelf organize media miscellany.**

BASIC AND BEAUTIFUL

above right **Ready-made gingerbread brackets dress up the basic coffee table for a cottage look and feel. Painted a crisp white, the table's details shine. Dual pulls of vintage-look green glass on each drawer layer on the style. Canvas "boxes" add storage and texture.**

simple beginnings
How would you revamp this table?

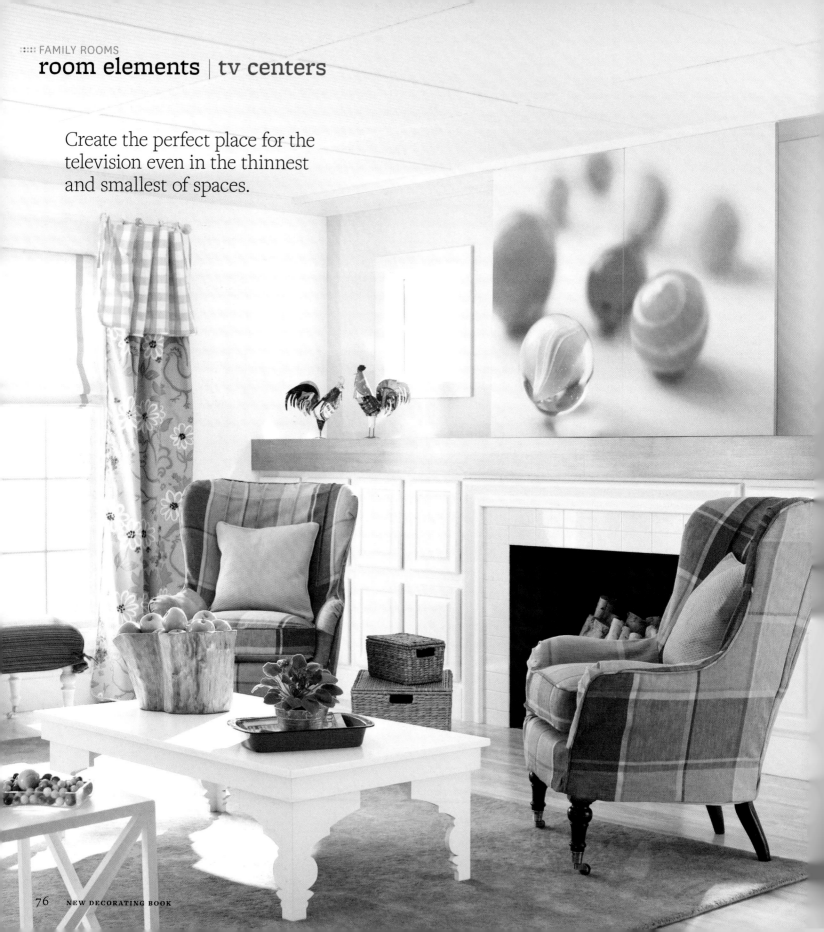

Create the perfect place for the
television even in the thinnest
and smallest of spaces.

FOR HIDDEN STYLE
opposite and above **It's easy to disguise the TV with sliding panels that look like a single piece of art.**

FOR MEDIA RESTRAINT
top left **Span a wall with low cabinets below the screen. The TV is set back from traffic, protecting it from damage.**

FOR FUN
top right **To incorporate a small TV into a room without making it the star, hang it above a wall of low-slung bookcases. The TV just blends in.**

FOR SMALL SPACES
middle left **Resist the urge to super-size the TV in a small room. Size screen and console to the room.**

FOR THE RIGHT FIT
middle right **Create a space in a wall of cabinets that exactly fits the TV so the screen looks built in.**

FOR SMART REUSE
bottom left **An old dresser repurposed to modern media storage has the clean lines suitable to today's screens.**

FOR FIREPLACE VIEWS
bottom right **Use the open real estate above the fireplace. Cabinets flanking the fireplace are useful for hiding media and game gear.**

get organized | media storage

Organize media- and game-related gear
using shelves, baskets, and bins.

STORE IN BULK
above left **A large ottoman
makes room for big game
pieces. A flatware caddy
offers compartments to
hold the smaller items.**

BE PREPARED
left **Gather extra
batteries, a disc-cleaning
kit, and microfiber cloths
for dusting the TV screen
and store them in a
basket where they're
easy to access.**

MARK IT
above right **Even pretty
boxes have to work to be
useful. Label every bin,
basket, and box so
everyone can easily find
everything and reliably
store it away.**

TAME IT
opposite **Save the space
around the TV for your
most often-used media
and put the overflow in
labeled bins stored
elsewhere. Keep gaming
remotes on a shallow tray
and place near the game
console but out of sight.**

TV to-dos
Shop for a new flat-panel TV with these tips in mind.

Mark the spot. Determine eye-level placement of your TV by sitting in the prime viewing spot or lying in bed. Have a helper mark the TV outline on the wall using painter's tape. The middle of the TV should be close to eye level; pick a TV that fits this spot.

Consider size. Bigger isn't necessarily better. Consider the dimensions of the room and where you sit relative to the TV. An oversize screen will overwhelm the room.

Viewing distance. A long-standing rule is that the best viewing distance is twice the screen's diagonal measurement. But with improved technology, you can sit farther away. At home, measure the distance from the TV to your viewing spot; view from that distance in the store to assess the picture's quality.

The best angle. Straight-on viewing is ideal. But flat panels, especially plasma TVs, have a wide viewing angle, so side viewing is less compromised.

kitchens

Today's kitchens are open 24-7. We want them to work hard and look good all the time. Here's how to make it happen.

10 Design Basics

1. THINK FUNCTION. Take notes while you're working in your kitchen. Will an island improve work flow? Would a new layout save you steps? Is there dining space? **2. OPT FOR DURABILITY** by choosing surface materials that are stain- and water-resistant, making them easy to clean. **3. WARM IT UP.** Counteract the cool metal of appliances with stained wood cabinetry, nubby textiles, and warm colors. **4. GO OUTSIDE THE BOX.** Use an old wood table for an island or place a settee at the table. Adapt a fun tablecloth for use as a window covering. These add charm and reduce the utilitarian feel. **5. MINIMIZE CABINETRY.** Remove some upper cabinets to help a small kitchen feel large—or replace solid cabinet doors with glass panels that expand the view. **6. ADD DETAILS.** Classic knobs, open shelves, and dramatic light fixtures change the kitchen's focus from all work to casual comfort. **7. GO SOFT.** Contrast a kitchen's smooth surfaces and hard edges with upholstered furniture and fabric window treatments. **8. STORE IN STYLE.** Hide kitchen clutter inside a pretty armoire or cabinet. Line shelves and drawers with patterned paper, and stack baskets inside a pantry. **9. COLOR UP.** Be adventurous. Paint one kitchen wall or an island in a bold color. Paint a pattern on the floor. Or use bright red chairs for seating at the island. **10. ACCESSORIZE** by bringing in mirrors, candlesticks, and table lamps that would look just as good in the living room.

styles we love

Wide-open floor plans invite the kitchen into living areas and everyone into the kitchen. Here's how to roll out the welcome mat.

NATURAL SELECTIONS

above left **Blend the best of Grandma's era and today with a stylish and functional kitchen. Use base cabinets to keep most items hidden while open upper cabinets let dishware play beautiful as well as useful roles. Shallow corner shelves maximize storage without impinging on counter space.**

COLORFUL CLASSIC

above right **Gutsy and strong, the orange wall and patchwork tiles in this kitchen addition deliver a color punch. Classic white cabinets soften the look to retro rather than kitsch. Painting one wall a bold color is a quick project that may be the perfect way to bring your kitchen out of the doldrums.**

COTTAGE REDUX

opposite left **A focal-point wall painted the color of sea glass turns this landlubbers' kitchen into a showplace. Beaded-board ceilings enhance the cottage style and would look good on a flat ceiling as well. Paint cabinetry white so it plays a supporting role to the painted wall.**

MODERN CASUAL

opposite right **A kitchen open to dining and living spaces must be handsome and hardworking. Handsome comes with exposed wood beams, wide-plank paneling, and concrete countertops. Soft shades of putty green on the cabinets and tile, along with checkered plywood flooring, quietly add color and definition to the space.**

Fast kitchen makeovers

A to-the-studs kitchen makeover is a big and expensive project. While you're saving up to remodel, paint can be an affordable way to inject a temporary style boost into the busiest room at home. Spruce up cabinetry. Dated cabinets are perfect candidates for this quick fix. Be sure to properly sand and prime the cabinets before applying the finish coat. It's important to note that today's primers even stick to laminate countertops. Although this is not a permanent solution, painted countertops should last up to five years. Add a pattern. Introduce pattern by stenciling one focal point wall. Look for updated stencils featuring geometric patterns in oversize scale. If the kitchen walls are small, try an oversize stencil on the floor. Vinyl flooring covers up easily with paint. If the vinyl floor is patterned, use the pattern as a textured background for the new stencil.

styles we love

VINTAGE BEACH
Crisp ocean blue swathes the cabinets, while brackets on upper cabinets, a farmhouse sink, and quilted tile behind the stove create a modern version of a beachhouse kitchen. Add cherry-stained flooring for a vintage 1930s style.

CLASSIC WHITE
above left Classic style is in the details: glass doors with muntins, island brackets, curved bases, X-shape wine dividers, and traditional cabinet hardware. It all adds up to a look that's up-to-date and timeless—perfect for a remodeling project in the most expensive-to-do room in the house.

CRAFTSMAN COLOR
above right Chartreuse cabinets and blue-gray window frames are an unexpected color duo, but they show one way creative pairings express style. The cabinet color plays off the green hand-glazed tiles, while the smoky blue complements the stone countertops. A walnut shelf seals the Arts and Crafts style.

Making kitchen space add up

A too-small kitchen offers a challenge. But you can make a small space feel—and work—bigger. Assess what your kitchen needs to hold, and discard what isn't critical before you start a makeover. Be ruthless. Remove as many upper cabinets as possible; replace the storage space with open shelves. Maximize wall space along a traffic zone by using readymade and shallow storage tools such as brackets, hangers, and hooks; install them from floor to ceiling. Capitalize on the headroom above an island by using it to store bulky pans on a hanging pot rack. Look for pullout storage racks to make use of deep cabinets and under-the-sink cupboards.

color palette

Gray is the easy-to-get-along-with neutral, but don't think of it as boring. These hues showcase the colorful side of gray.

pearl gray, a lavender-tinted gray, is sophisticated and dramatic. **Try it:** inside a charcoal-painted cabinet.

wheat taupe, a grayed natural tone, looks rich and elegant paired with black. **Try it:** on chairs pulled up to a black table.

misty blue, soothing and cool, makes an elegant statement. **Try it:** on the ceiling.

gray sage, a perfect complement to cream, looks great on walls. **Try it:** on breakfast room walls with a ceiling painted misty blue.

satin silver, subtle and warm, fills a room with light. **Try it:** on cabinetry instead of pure white.

Color mastery

Learn how to incorporate gray, an adaptable neutral, into any scheme.

Make a choice. Gray is the neutral's neutral. Its many shades harmonize with most any color partner. Use a gray palette in rooms that go from rustic to romantic.

Start with the dark. To find color companions for gray, look at the darkest color on the gray paint card to find the undertone. For gray with blue undertones, pair it with a muted powder blue. If it has green undertones, pair it with a muted sage.

Warmer ahead. Not-so-perfect pieces, such as weathered woods and worn metals, warm and soften even the coolest of grays.

Find the glow. Combine a soft gray wall with pieces in cream and white to make the gray almost shimmer.

Expand the palette. Choose warm and cool grays to give a room added dimension, such as blue-gray on the ceiling and warm gray on the crown molding.

before & after

Fed up with a galley kitchen? A small addition provides a big change: extra space for eating and storage. New cabinets in a warm brown tone mix with stainless-steel shelves to ban the tunnel effect of the old kitchen.

BEFORE
3 common flaws

1 White cabinets are worn and inefficient.

2 Busy stripes of floor tile look out of place.

3 Too little light makes kitchen feel crowded.

AFTER
3 fabulous fixes

1 Wood cabinets with wood pulls provide a smooth, sleek look.

2 Floor tiles laid in a flame-stitch pattern add personality.

3 Larger windows and reflective countertops spread the light.

Try this!
Add contrasting accents such as blue jars and chairs to brighten neutrals.

Keeping focus

Small kitchens work best when there's a clear plan for function and style.

Linear thinking. Beaded-board walls and ceiling add texture and interest to plain white walls. And the walls contrast with the medium-tone wood cabinets, adding to the feeling of airiness.

Elbowroom. Moving the range across the room opened up generous counter space flanking the sink to make prep and cleanup easier.

Material evidence. Adding just a few feet to the far end of this kitchen and opening up the corner provided plenty of storage and a new counter space perfect for a home office.

Enough and no more. The new space allowed for more lower cabinets. Upper cabinets were kept to a minimum because the storage wasn't needed, and the open space makes the room feel larger.

Neutral zone. A palette of soft, creamy white and midtone woods combined with flat cabinet fronts keeps the kitchen looking perpetually neat.

style made simple | small islands

Your kitchen might be too small for a big island, but any kitchen will work harder and look better with a slim workhorse.

SMOOTH OPERATOR
left **Jars and bottles are neatly organized in a stained-to-match wood box on the bottom shelf of this slim island. Drawer glides installed on the bottom of the box ensure easy and safe access.**

SIDE WISE
above left **Success is in the details: A two-tier hanging rack makes room for spices, and a utility hook holds measuring spoons. The spatula-and-spoon basket is an accessory for a commercial-grade hanging rack system.**

THE GREEN MACHINE
above right **This 4×2-foot unfinished island packs in function with a shelf added to the island's side rails and an undermount wire basket drawer installed under the top. Repurposed wine racks hold kitchen gear. And the island gets style with a green stain finish— perfect for its country kitchen setting.**

Try this!
Add an accent by choosing black window sashes in white frames.

ROLLING STEEL

No room for a pantry? Create well-ordered kitchen storage in pockets of space, such as on this rolling island. A work surface on top and two handy shelves filled with staples and bowls roll to wherever you're working. The rail around the bottom shelf keeps things in place when you're on the move.

Try this!
Use a vintage bracket under an island overhang for classic cottage style.

BREAD

RETRO REFLECTION
Milky green subway tile reflects the owner's favorite kitchen collectibles and accents basic white cabinets.

Stainproof and style-savvy, ceramic tile is a kitchen's best remodeling secret.

FLOOR BORDER
top left **Subway tile wraps around the cabinetry for a look that's both classic and new-fashioned.**

STYLE SETTERS
top right **Boldly colored tiles extend the cabinets' green from the counter up to the ceiling.**

EYE-CATCHERS
middle left **An intricate tile pattern transforms any wall into a focal point. Break up the print with shelves and cabinets.**

CLASSIC STYLE
middle right **White subway tile is the go-to element for any kitchen. It's as classic and stylish as a basic white shirt.**

GREEN WITH ENVY
bottom left **Just one wall of tile in this heavenly chartreuse delivers a color punch that wakes up a snoozy space.**

HEARTH HOME
bottom right **A favorite quilt pattern inspired the tile treatment around the range. Note how the trim edges the backsplash.**

get organized | pantries

Need a pantry? It's as simple as adapting a piece of furniture or as clever as reworking a closet.

Try this!
Gather a favorite collection on a cabinet top.

RETRO CHARM
above left **A vintage Hoosier cabinet offers storage for kitchen gear and deep drawers for bulky items. Glass-front cabinets on the top keep pretty linens and china in view even when they're not in use.**

STORAGE GIANT
above right **A swath of square footage tucked behind solid doors illustrates quantity storage that's hidden. Wire baskets on drawer glides keep cans and spices corralled and at your fingertips. Leaving the bottom open makes room for larger items.**

TUCKED AWAY
opposite left **This 4×7-foot larder keeps countertop appliances and food handy on shelves that wrap around the space. Wider shelves at the bottom and back allow for storage of bulk items, while shallower shelves above keep everyday items in plain sight.**

COOK'S CENTRAL
opposite right **Love to bake? Outfit a dedicated armoire with the necessary ingredients, appliances, and utensils. Even the inside of the doors can go to work with cork and chalkboard inserts to keep track of household activities and shopping lists.**

Right sizing

Pantries can be an afterthought in some modern homes. If yours lacks a pantry, consider turning an armoire or hutch into dedicated kitchen storage. And if your house does have a pantry that's basically a small closet, be sure the space is designed for maximum utility for your needs. *Take inventory first.* Knowing what you'll be storing in the pantry will help determine how to equip the space with shelves and baskets of the right size and placement. *Allow for access.* If your new pantry is freestanding, be sure to allow yourself enough room to open the door (or doors) completely and to access shelves and drawers without the doors bumping into nearby cabinets or tables.

bathrooms

Need a place to destress, recharge, or invigorate? Dip your toe into our pool of ideas for planning a stylish, functional bath that meets all your needs.

10 Design Basics

1. INVEST IN YOUR FOCAL POINT. Is it a furniture-look vanity, massaging shower body sprays, or marble tile walls? Take the plunge on an item with lasting appeal. **2. CREATE SPACE WITH COLOR.** Pale walls make a small bath feel airy; dark hues add cozy depth. An accent color on the ceiling draws eyes upward, as does vertical-stripe wallpaper or beaded-board paneling on walls. **3. MATCH METALLICS.** Use one finish for the faucet, showerhead, towel bars, and hardware. **4. PATTERN THE FLOOR.** Floor tile in an all-over mosaic pattern or as a colorful inset border adds interest. **5. ADD FURNITURE.** If you have the space, tuck in a slipper chair, add a small dresser for storage, or place a ceramic garden stool by the tub to hold a candle, novel, or toiletries. **6. SOFTEN HARD EDGES** by hanging a soft Roman shade or laying down a nubby rug. **7. TRADE OUT TILE.** Add interest to plain tiles by replacing a row with colorful glass mosaics or patterned ceramic ones. **8. REFLECT ON THE MIRROR.** A bamboo-frame mirror adds sophistication to a traditional bath; a brushed-metal frame offers a cool, modern vibe. **9. ADD FLATTERING, BALANCED LIGHT** with sconces or pendants flanking the vanity mirror—lights above the mirror cast unflattering shadows. **10. USE DURABLE MATERIALS.** Shop for water-resistant, vinyl-clad windows (especially in a shower), resilient sheet flooring, and mildew-blocking primer and paint.

styles we love

Create personality in the smallest room in the house. Get playful with color and surfaces. Be serious about amenities that organize and pamper.

EVERYDAY ELEGANT
above left **Swap a boxy vanity for a piece with furniture-style details. It makes a bath more comfortable and homelike. Home centers and their websites are good sources for dresser-style vanities. Balance the vanity's finish with a shower curtain that plays up the color and look— here it's a rich paisley— and match the metallic finish of its knobs in the fixtures and accessories.**

FIT FOR RETRO
above right **Rewrite the history of a dark, cramped vintage bath with an airy, space-making redo. Access natural light with frosted glass in the door. Light bounces off the clean, white surfaces—marble tiles in the shower, ceramic tiles on walls, and hexagonal mosaic tiles on the floor. A rounded half-wall implies more elbowroom. A pedestal sink demands little floor space and preserves vintage charm.**

URBAN WOODLAND
opposite left **Nature needn't be harsh. This "earthy urban" bath is a sophisticated mix of sculptural forms with a chunky sink atop a walnut open-leg console, and whimsical touches such as wallpaper depicting a hand-drawn forest. Dark-stained wood flooring grounds the space; humble, unpolished metals—a slim raw-steel table and a brushed-nickel faucet— add understated patina.**

TWEAKED TRADITIONAL
opposite right **Resist the urge to purge original bath features (refinishing will brighten a sink or tub). Use the colors or style to inspire a new look. The vintage pink and cream mosaic floor tiles of this 1929 bath inspired its new toile wallpaper (OK in a bath without a shower). The new tub taps match the sink's cross-handle originals. This pedestal sink opens floor space but has the right heft.**

Live large in half the space

A half bath may sound compact, but smart product selection maximizes every inch. Embrace open space. The more open space the eye can see, the bigger the room feels. A vanity with an open, table-like base, for instance, provides a view of the floor to create the sense of a larger space. Pedestal sinks or ultra-modern wall-hung consoles are also wise choices. Millwork makes magic. Don't underestimate the impact of molding. Opt for tall baseboards and crown molding in a light color to stretch ceiling height. Basic design choices always work. Pale, safe color schemes, especially neutrals, make a room feel less crowded. A mirror is a small space's best friend, reflecting light, adding depth to a room, and providing a focal point.

styles we love

TRUE GRIT
Get a vintage farmhouse
look without sacrificing
must-have conveniences.
This antique farm table
became a double-basin
vanity with a durable zinc
countertop, towel bars, and
shelving. Select quartersawn
wood—it's less likely to
buckle in wet areas—and
coat it with urethane for
floors. For the look of
antique glass, simply hang a
stained-glass panel in front
of an existing window.

Try this!
Update sconces by attaching fabric to self-stick shades.

VINTAGE COTTAGE

above left **Touches of black keep a cottage bath from appearing too sweet. Here, black-tile flowers are scattered into the design of a hexagonal tile floor. Black bands define a Roman shade. Enlist containers with black accents, such as black-rimmed enamel buckets. Iron towel hooks and bars punctuate the look.**

REFINED RUSTIC

above right **When a dropped ceiling was removed, wood beams were revealed. That inspired the room's "opposites attract" strategy of pairing rustic with refined. The floor is unglazed tumbled stone; the walls are a clay-and-plaster mix; and the vanity is a retrofitted limed-wood cabinet. Curling-vine lights and a shapely silver-patina mirror frame supply graceful touches.**

Storage solutions

Organize your bath to make your morning routine less hectic. Retrofit for added space. In the cabinets, for example, add pullout trays, hampers, waste cans, and drawer organizers. Create a storage ledge by adding a narrow shelf above a pedestal sink or alongside a tub. Use between-stud space to carve out a recessed area for a new storage or medicine cabinet. Bring in storage basics. Install hooks for towels below a window or on the back of the bathroom door. Squeeze in a storage ottoman to hold bulky hair-grooming appliances and to provide seating.

color palette

Is it green? Is it blue? Whatever you call it, this sea glass-inspired hue brings a soothing, spa-like lull to a busy bath or living space.

eucalyptus, bold and bracing, is best used in smaller doses. **Try it:** in a powder room.

pale cloud, white with a whisper of blue, subtly soothes a room. **Try it:** in a master bath or bedroom.

celadon, with subtle yellowish-green and black undertones, provides a highly sophisticated look. **Try it:** with ivory upholstery and soft black furnishings.

seafoam, with a gentle blue undertone, imparts an upbeat, "clear-sky day" personality. **Try it:** paired with off-white wainscoting and trim in any room.

sweet mint, with a gentle, bluish-green undertone, establishes a restful feel. **Try it:** for wall and bedding colors in a master suite or on a bath ceiling.

Color mastery

Like an ocean's spray, this watered-down blue-green offers calmness and serenity—which is why you see it in spas and beach resorts. Capture its tranquillity in your bath with these tips:

Sea side. Car siding installed horizontally and painted soft celadon adds a laid-back beach cabana look to this powder room.

Penny wise. As copper ages, it develops a verdigris patina. Use this natural pairing as inspiration for your bath's fixtures. In this bath, an oil-rubbed bronze faucet and sconces add depth and warmth.

Color mediation. Seafoam can be a challenge to match in surfaces and accessories. Mosaic tiles, however, can be a blend of three or four similar and harmonious colors. Use a mosaic tile in a seafoam blend of blues and greens to unify the similar yet not exact shades of your shower curtain, towels, and wall paint.

Work with wood. In a room outfitted in oak-stained cabinets or red pine floors, choose a sea glass-inspired wall paint with yellow undertones. For a bath with a white cabinet or pedestal sink, shop for a version that has blue-black undertones.

Try this!
Add a dowel between brackets to double a shelf's function.

before & after

Instead of a budget-busting remodel, give a style-sagging 5×9-foot bath a facelift. Use these simple cosmetic cures that can be completed in about a weekend.

BEFORE

3 common flaws

1 Dull-tone walls and a plain shower curtain make the room look tired and timeworn.

2 An outdated bath cabinet cramps the room, and a barren mirror suffers from style anemia.

3 A lack of storage makes everyday use of the room inconvenient.

3 fabulous fixes

1 Spring-green paint and a lively print shower curtain add color.

2 A pedestal sink pays homage to the bath's style roots. A new mirror frame also better suits the style.

3 A bench, wall cabinet, and several hooks offer seating and storage.

FOCUS ON THE POSITIVE

opposite **The vintage white tub and tile walls were in good shape and would function as solid, neutral foundations for the style upgrade. The wiring for lights was in the right place, so new sconces and a sparkly chandelier were installed. The sink, too, was well placed. Simply swapping out a dark, bulky vanity with a white pedestal sink added much-needed air and floor space.**

FRAME UP

above left **A new wide frame for the mirror adds substance and supplies a ledge for toiletries. This one was custom-made, but simply search the Internet for mirror-frame kits to find similar options. New brushed-nickel fixtures for the sink and tub now brighten the bathroom.**

COLOR SPOTS

above right **The walls spring to new life with a coat of fresh paint in spring green. Tile was refreshed with a splash of color by chipping out a few tiles and popping in green samples from a tile shop. A line of silver coat hooks was inset among new mosaic tiles below a new cabinet.**

Try this!
Add crystal handles and ribbed-glass panels to a cabinet for extra sparkle.

style made simple | 1 vanity 3 ways

Let your basic bath with its standard-issue oak vanity soak up new personality and purpose with easy additions.

bare canvas With a simple, solid form, this vanity is easy to update.

TRADITION TRIUMPH

opposite **Gray-brown paint creates a sophisticated, furniturelike look for the plain vanity. Decorative Colonial-style feet applied to the toe-kick add to the illusion. The faucet, light fixture, and mirror in oil-rubbed bronze continue the look. (Go for a mirror that makes a glam statement.) An étagère squeezes storage into a few feet of floor space. Display the pretty stuff (try clear acrylic kitchen canisters) and stash the rest in stylish baskets and boxes.**

MODERN MAGIC

above left **Mimic lacquered furniture by coating the vanity in a durable, high-gloss alkyd enamel paint. This curtain's chain link motif repeats in C-shape door pulls. Recruit items from other areas of the house to service the bath—a kitchen utensils rail to stow grooming supplies, and a white-metal magazine rack to organize towels. Tie it all up with fixtures in a brushed-metal finish.**

RURAL ROUTE

above right **Go with the grain of the vanity's oak finish for a farmhouse look. The mirror is built from salvaged barnwood for rugged texture. The galvanized exterior lights and zinc gate pulls used as cabinet hardware are from farm-supply stores and home centers. Complete the look with beaded board hung horizontally on the walls and a ticking-stripe shower curtain.**

Try this!
Use a shiny, galvanized bucket from the hardware store to hold fresh towels.

room elements | shower curtains

Shake up a generic bath with one easy addition: a new shower curtain. It's a simple redecorating project—and inexpensive. Choose one that matches your style.

Try this!
Use a hotel-style nylon liner that's mildew-resistant and washable.

A TAILORED TAKE
Dress up a waffle-weave shower curtain with a no-sew valance made from a table runner (install grommets in the runner before attaching). Use fusible webbing to attach the runner to the curtain and to add rows of black cotton twill tape.

A TWIST ON TRADITION

top left **Turn a richly patterned tablecloth into a country French shower curtain. Choose a cloth with dimensions similar to a shower liner (about 72×72 inches). Hang it from shower curtain rings with clips.**

CREATIVE COTTAGE

top right **Turn a beloved floral curtain into your shower curtain. Hang two panels from shower rings with clips or, if using rings with loops or hooks, install grommets along each panel's top edge. Hem to the proper length.**

AN ECLECTIC EDGE

middle left **Dressmaker details—piping, button-trimmed loops—lend polish to a shower panel made from affordable quilter's fabric in a free-spirited update of paisley.**

SEASIDE SPA

middle right **Embellish a natural hemp shower curtain with strands of capiz shell. Tie the strands to the shower curtain loops. Hand stitch the strands to the curtain at intervals to stabilize.**

BOHEMIAN BATH

bottom left **Layer upon layer of ruffles gives this curtain the flirtacious spirit of a flamenco skirt. With a curtain this show-offish, choose a solid-color fabric and use it in a bath with a simple vanity and tile.**

REGAL REFINEMENT

bottom right **For a curtain that's part tapestry, part humble quilt, stitch together elegant cloth napkins in uniform sizes.**

get organized | bath closet

Is your family's bath the scene of a rush-hour traffic jam each morning? Streamline its storage—and add peace of mind—with these organization strategies.

GRAB AND GO
left **Fill handled containers based on function. Create caddies for manicure tools, cleaning supplies, and medications. Bath storage is about accessibility. Anything you use regularly must be in a container at your fingertips—versus hidden in the dark back of the closet.**

TAKE A SPIN
above left **A lazy Susan prevents small items from getting lost at the back of a shelf. Line shelves with plastic-coated fabric for quick cleanups. Repurpose containers, such as these acrylic dry-goods canisters and cooking oil flasks labeled with new adhesive letters.**

BUCKET LIST
above right **Assign each family member a bucket to hold personal grooming supplies. The buckets are easily toted from closet to sink to tub and back. Designate spots to hang the buckets as well as hooks for towels and robes by attaching metal and adhesive-back hooks inside cabinet and closet doors.**

THE BIG PICTURE
Make organization part of your daily routine. Start with a metal-frame, three-bag laundry sorter. Dangle a stain-treater on a ribbon to deal with messy garments before tossing them in a bin.

Darks *Lights* *Delicates*

Try this!
Quiet a busy bath's hectic pace with soothing blue walls.

work spaces

Organized. Versatile. Stylish. Let those three descriptive words define the work spaces and storage areas anywhere in your home.

10 Design Basics

1. PLAY WITH COLOR. A playful attitude using lighthearted colors and patterns can take the drudgery out of any kind of work. **2. MAKE IT PERSONAL** by providing space for favorite collections and a bulletin board. Hang family photos on the wall. **3. BE COMFY.** Use a comfortable desk chair and add guest seating. Make sure you can reach storage with ease. Control sound with fabrics and rugs. **4. IMAGINE THE CLUTTER.** Think about where piles are most likely to accumulate. Then plan storage places that are easy to use so stuff gets put away. **5. MAKE ROOM** for multiuse opportunities: Capitalize on space to add a second chair to a desk or room around a worktable for family members. Provide an in-box for every family member. **6. ADD COUNTERS.** Consider providing counters to ease tasks such as folding clothing or wrapping packages. **7. PLUG IN.** Plan for placement and number of electrical outlets and switches. Think about where cords will be exposed and include ways to hide them. **8. SCALE DOWN.** Clear out the excess stuff before you start buying storage pieces. **9. UNIFY MULTITASKING.** If a room will serve two completely separate uses—guest room and office, for example—create a plan that blends the uses with a single style. **10. LIGHT RIGHT.** Appropriate lighting—especially well-placed task lighting—is key to making an area function well.

styles we love

Style and productivity go hand in hand. Having a comfortable, attractive space to work makes you more efficient.

MODERN TRAVELER
above left **This is an office? A wall of storage cubes holds travel keepsakes and favorite books. Office clutter gets hidden in covered boxes stacked against a backdrop of caramel-color walls. The glass-top desk all but disappears, an especially smart idea for a work surface in a small space.**

SPARE CLASSIC
above right **Curves on the desk reflect a fun-loving riff on classic furniture design. Snuggling a stylish desk and chair into the corner of a beautiful living room makes a handy spot for catching up on e-mail and paying bills. With wireless access and a slim laptop computer, there's no need for cords.**

LITTLE BIT COUNTRY
opposite left **Handsome enough for an entry space, this built-in desk by the home's back door makes room for two, accommodates file storage in the base cabinets, and holds office gear in open cubbies. The real organizer is a charging center ready to power up all sorts of handheld devices, keeping them fully charged and at hand when family members head out the door.**

YOUNG AND FUNKY
opposite right **Lime green and citrusy orange deliver a style punch that injects fun into every work project. So, too, does the leggy desk that serves as a dressing table when the room doubles as a guest room. The color-framed bulletin board draws attention with an artsy feel while keeping the family organized.**

Office basics

Consider these work-smart options. Desktop Plan a desk height of 26 inches for a computer keyboard and 30 inches for a crafting table. If you have room for only one work surface, install the desktop at the higher measurement and add a pullout keyboard shelf beneath it. Storage Standard filing cabinets provide efficient storage. Use a closet with pullout bins to organize bulky supplies such as printer paper. Tall cabinets add vertical interest and storage without hogging floor space. Seating Save your back. Use an office chair with lumbar support if you're going to spend a lot of time at the desk. Lighting Plan for overall lighting and specialized task lighting. To cut glare on computer monitors, use adjustable desk lamps, general lighting on dimmers, and floor lamps that bounce light off the ceiling. Message Boards Organize family schedules with chalkboards for messages and bulletin boards to hold calendars.

styles we love

CRAFTING CORNER

Bright blue walls, overscale pattern, and framed artwork add joy to this work space. A table made from purchased metal legs, a stock kitchen cabinet, and a plywood top adds efficiency. A roll of crafts paper protects the desk during projects, while stools and chairs offer a range of seating heights for kids to adults.

Try this!
Turn clean empty cans into supply caddies by wrapping them with art paper.

SEW ZONE

above left **A movable island cabinet is a mobile workhorse, thanks to casters. Consider these ideas: magnetic spice tins and a thread organizer keep buttons and spools handy, a cutting mat protects the countertop, sliding shelves provide easy access to supplies and heavier machines or tools, and a vintage frame showcases idea swatches.**

ART CENTER

above right **Kids are drawn to art and crafts projects, so make it easy to let them play, with supervision, of course. This well-stocked art room sized down for kids is just a few feet from the kitchen island. A roomy utility sink at a kid-friendly height makes cleanup easy. Open shelves keep everything organized and in view.**

Contain the mess

A crafts space should be organized, yet messes can quickly take over. Here's how to keep it tidy. Sort it. Trays in various shapes and sizes can hold almost anything. Use them on desktops and in closets. Stack it. Think vertically; choose boxes and bins that stack on top of each other to maximize space. Post it. Gather notes, dates, and photos on bulletin or magnetic boards. File it. Stash fabric swatches, instructions, and project ideas in files to keep handy near the tabletop. Store it. Provide separate storage for seldom-used items. Unless you use something daily, pack it up and store it away.

Cozy orange holds rooms in a warm embrace. Dial down the brightness and pair it with blue-gray for a trendy duo.

turmeric, a classic golden tan, bridges strong oranges with neutrals. **Try it:** on walls paired with white trim.

wild fire, with red tones, has heat and strength. Try it: on a chair at a white desk.

carrot stick, a fresh vegetable hue, packs personality. **Try it:** stenciled on a laundry wall.

zinnia, a sun-kissed orange, reveals red and yellow in the mix. Try it: with oh-so-chic pale teal.

pumpkin seed, with yellow undertones to lighten, is perfect for walls. **Try it:** in kids' rooms—of course!

Color mastery

Learn how to decorate using this hip, hot blast of a color.

Tone it brown. Mitigate orange's shock value by picking a shade with some brown in it. To assess how toned down the orange should be, gather a collection of chips from pure to muddy, then select the muddier ones. Try a sample to make sure you love the hue.

Pick a room. Use orange in a contained room such as an office or laundry so the strong color doesn't overwhelm adjoining spaces.

Find companions. Hot pink, pale pink, teal blue, olive green, and robin's egg blue all offer good orange pairings. Look for a combination of colors in fabric or wallpaper. Beware of black or you may think it's always Halloween.

Start slow. Unsure of orange? Introduce it as a bit player in accessories and fabrics. Bring home a bouquet of orange flowers to start the selection process.

Try this!
Slipcover a chair back with a fabric pocket.

ORANGE REVEALED
A floral fabric splashed with ruddy blossoms provides color impact and a hide-the-clutter curtain for this closet turned office. Orange accessories dial up the energy.

before & after | office

Spare bedrooms aren't toss-away spaces. Turn them into home office and guest room combinations using wise furniture choices and classic architectural details. It's only fitting for their open-all-hours flexibility.

BEFORE
3 common flaws

1   Makeshift desk has no storage space.

2   Boxy space is bland in white, white, white.

3   A large sofa bed gobbles up precious floor space.

3 fabulous fixes

1 A small-scale office armoire conceals desk space and storage.

2 A molding strip and a two-tone paint treatment create the look of wainscoting.

3 A sleeper chair and storage ottoman maximize space and open for guests.

Try this!
Hang artwork on the inside of armoire doors.

HANDSOME STORAGE

opposite **A bookcase cabinet holds office essentials on the right and guest room items on the left. Wrapping paper lines the glass and hides its contents. Sliding doors save space because furniture can cozy right up to the cabinet. Outfit the cabinet interior with baskets for organized storage you can grab and take to the desk.**

OPEN SESAME

above left **It almost feels magical to shoehorn a super-efficient office into a space that moonlights as a guest room. The trick is finding a desk armoire that includes file storage, a pullout keyboard tray, and desk space for a computer. Closed, the cabinet hides its hardworking function.**

DETAILS THAT ADD UP

above right **Black-and-white photos in colorful mats decorate the inside of the armoire doors. Hang the pictures with easy-release adhesive strips so you can change images as desired. The nearby end table with CD drawers serves as bedside table and deskside storage.**

get organized | office supplies

Eliminate paper avalanches at your house by turning one corner of a room into a super-organized work center with storage space to spare.

THINK AHEAD

left **It's easy to lose your concentration on a trip to the kitchen. Create a mini snack bar in the office complete with labeled containers for favorites. Make the labels using dry-erase markers on vinyl-coated paper.**

SORT BY SIZE

above left **Insert flexible dividers into drawers so you can sort and store easily. Use covered boxes to hold a jumble of items such as computer cords. Always label what's undercover and out of plain sight.**

GROUP LIKES WITH LIKES

above right **Create a printing center with room for the printer and a stash of paper within easy reach. If your cabinet has a closed back, drill a hole to allow access to an electrical outlet. Reserve the top shelf for art supplies and paints on a lazy Susan.**

Try this! Use a column of stacking magazine racks to organize file folders.

OFFICE CENTRAL
Set up a power work center with shallow cabinets and a desk. This desk hutch is made of four wall shelves (two hung horizontally, two vertically). Closet components form a bank of cabinets.

style made simple | desks

Not every home has enough space for a dedicated office, but it's possible to make room for a desk almost anywhere using one of these options.

CORNER OFFICE

above left **Transform an unused bedroom corner into a pretty writing center. A floor lamp gives good overall lighting without eating up desktop space. Use a clear glass blotter to protect the desktop and slip favorite photos and artwork under its surface.**

HIDEAWAY DESK

above right **When closed, this piece of furniture looks like a handsome cabinet. Opened, it reveals a secret: It's a desk complete with a work surface that flips open and a filing cabinet in the base. The cork lamp base makes a good-looking bulletin board.**

STORAGE TO GO

opposite left **A table makes a great work surface, but what about storage? Make your own by adding shelves, boxes, and baskets all around. Create storage that's easy to adapt as your work needs change: Even a tote can keep papers and supplies at hand.**

COMMUTER SPACE

opposite right **A desk on casters offers the ultimate in office flexibility. To make one like this, attach a premade countertop to a pair of rolling file drawer units. Stack file folders on a zigzag shelf that rests on the desktop. When work is done, just roll the unit into a corner.**

Just for you

It's your work space. That's the perfect reason for making it match your style. Start with a desk that fits. Look for a desk that offers the kind of storage and work space you need, the style you want. Display your style. Paint the wall you'll view at the desk a favorite hue. For an office tucked into a corner of another room, select folders, notebooks, and other accessories in a favorite color. Use patterns to add interest and make it personal; select wallpaper or contact paper to make or cover accessories.

styles we love | laundries

Give your laundry room a fresh look that makes you feel good while you work.

UPSTYLE UPSTAIRS

above left **A corner of the attic might seem like a less-than-optimal spot for a laundry, but the right decor can make it work. Paint surfaces a bright white. Flank a handsome washer and dryer with beaded board and top with a counter for function. Installing a shelf at the back keeps supplies handy. A counter-height table provides folding space.**

OLD STYLE

above right **This brand-new utility room has a ton of vintage appeal, but there's nothing old-fashioned about how hard it works. Slate countertops resist scratches, and the wood floor has a distressed paint finish that camouflages dirt. Neutral shades of ocher and gray in the space create a relaxing atmosphere.**

BASEMENT BEAUTY

opposite left **The extra square footage in a basement makes perfect sense for a laundry room. Here's how to make it look good: Hang indoor/outdoor curtain panels to cover the cement block, top front-loading machines with a table for folding and stacking, accessorize with soap-filled containers, and bring in a freestanding sink cabinet.**

HIDEAWAY UTILITY

opposite right **A laundry center hidden behind closed doors and topped with a counter for folding can be tucked into almost any space in a house. Cabinets above and on both sides add hanging space for clothing and storage for cleaning gear.**

Makeovers on a budget

All work and no style can make a laundry dull. Here's how to pour on the freshness without spending a fortune. Paint it bright. It's the least expensive option and the surest way to lighten the look and erase dirt. An all-over coat is great, but for a little personal style consider painting stripes vertically or horizontally around the room. Introduce pattern. A framed print on the wall, an indoor-outdoor rug on the floor, and patterned labels on bins reflect what you love. Light it right. This is a work zone, so make sure to provide pendant or undercabinet lighting that can help you see the stains. Store in style. A single shelf with baskets lined with washable canvas looks good while keeping stain removers and specialized cleaners handy.

before & after

A laundry in a closet with bifold doors might be handy, but is hardly inspiring. Get a clean start by painting the walls a happy color and adding shelves and countertop.

BEFORE

3 common flaws

1 Storage is inefficient for laundry supplies.

2 Clumsy bifold doors get in the way.

3 A bland backdrop makes washday dull.

3 fabulous fixes

1 Use wall-to-wall shelves to hold laundry gear.

2 Replace doors with a roll-out-of-the-way blind and curvy valance.

3 Spend a little on paint and spread the sunshine.

Try this!
Edge a laundry room shelf with clothespins glued in place.

SHELF RELIEF

opposite **Maximize efficiency in a small laundry with a shelf that stretches from side to side. There's plenty of space for laundry detergents, stain removers, and other laundry equipment. For additional space, some appliance manufacturers offer tray-shape countertops to fit their front loaders.**

SHADY COVER-UP

above left **A wide window shade replaces clumsy closet doors and allows access to the entire laundry closet. A scalloped valance on the top of the door opening hides the roller mechanism. Consider a Roman shade as another option for hiding the laundry area from view.**

CLEVER CARE

above right **Consider these smart solutions for laundry duties: An outdoor retractable clothesline is always ready for action; it pulls out to attach to the opposite wall. A wire holder makes room to hang both iron and board inside the closet. A notched cutout in the counter allows the board to fit. A flip-top trash container collects lint.**

get organized | laundries

Make room for laundry chores and much more by maximizing a former walk-in closet with built-ins. Smart placement and stylish choices make it work.

DESIGN DETAILS

left **Hardworking spaces can also look good. Consider a solid-surfacing top for durability and beauty, elegant brackets to hold up shelves, and hand-forged iron pieces to contain paper supplies.**

STEAM IT UP

above left **Open this top drawer, and out pulls a nifty small-space solution: a built-in ironing board. Use it to add a little extra counter space for big projects, and store it away when not in use.**

UTILITY SOAK

above right **A stainless-steel, apron-front sink provides plenty of room for soaking soiled clothes or cleaning up after repotting a houseplant. Incorporating other household tasks in the same space as a washer and dryer is much more efficient and cost-effective because utilities are consolidated in a single space.**

WORK ZONES
Front-loading washers
and dryers slide under a
counter to allow for a
large work surface; the
center bin stores
detergents and other
laundry supplies. Shelves
and drawers above the
counter keep crafts
supplies within
easy reach.

bedrooms

In a 24-7 world of digital distractions and multitasking, having a soft place to land each night can soothe your soul.

10 Design Basics

1. START WITH THE MAIN FEATURE by placing the bed first and point it to face the best view—of a window, pretty furniture piece, or wall arrangement. **2. DON'T GET SQUEEZED.** Allow at least 2 feet of empty floor space on three sides of the bed for easy bed making; keep 3 to 4 feet clear in front of a closet, dresser, or door for dressing and traffic space. **3. LIGHT SWITCHES.** For elegance, trade a bedside table lamp for a petite crystal pendant light or swap out a ceiling fixture for a chandelier. **4. MAKE A GETAWAY.** A chair, ottoman, and lamp in a room corner or by a window create a quiet retreat. **5. INCLUDE FOOTNOTES.** Place comfortable seating— an upholstered bench or settee—at the foot of your bed. **6. GROW CLOSET SPACE** with built-in cabinets beside a window or door, storage ottomans, or an armoire to increase clothes storage. **7. GIVE 'EM THE SLIP.** Cover a tired headboard and footboard with pretty fabric slipcovers. **8. CHANGE THE SHEETS.** Rotate bedding by the season. Choose cool, breathable natural fibers such as cotton and silk for hot summer nights, snuggly flannel sheets and woolen blankets for winter. **9. DO A DOUBLE-TAKE.** A reversible comforter gives two looks for the money and a nice shot of color or pattern when the top is folded down. **10. SAVE SPACE.** Hang a shelf in place of a bedside table and a sconce in place of a lamp.

styles we love

Dream a bedtime story with a happy ending: a sleeping space that's pretty, practical, and personal. Choose your favorite from these diverse styles.

Try this!
Layer a patterned rug over sisal for a small hit of color on the floor.

GRACIOUS WOODLAND

above left **Let go of your perception that wood paneling is too rustic, burly, or old-fashioned. Choose a wood in a light-blond finish and let its rich graining provide a clean, contemporary backdrop for slick lacquered tables and aged metallic accessories. Soften the space with an upholstered settee at the foot of the bed and plump pillows in bold geometric and nature motifs.**

COOL TRADITIONAL

above right **Antique creamware plates are unlikely, but eye-catching, art above the bed in this room where a limited palette of blue and cream creates a cohesive look. Yellow undertones in the bedding, table skirt, and caned chair coordinate with the plates. To update a traditional space like this, trade draperies for matchstick blinds.**

CONTEMPO COTTAGE

opposite left **When you keep the cottage-base foundations of a room clean and simple—cream-painted paneling, trim, and furniture, for instance—you can easily mix in hot home decor trends by swapping out the bedding and accessories. Here, an exotic Moroccan trend shows up in the poppy-and-blue bedding and lampshade.**

SUITE MODERN

opposite right **Black can be bold and modern, but turns feminine as iron curlicues on a bed, curvy legs on a table, and billowy stripes on curtains. Unsure where to start adding black? Begin with small touches, such as piping on a pillow or frames for art. Or be fearless: Paint window sashes in a glossy ebony.**

Guest services

Think like a four-star hotel by stocking your guest room with pampering extras. Make your own minibar by filling a basket with chocolate bars, bags of nuts, and other packaged snacks. Set up a morning coffee bar on a small table; equip it with a small coffeemaker, mugs, and an assortment of coffees, teas, and cocoas. Stock a night table drawer with itty-bitty versions of favorite toiletries. Include a laminated card with your household Wi-Fi password and an easy-access spot for plugging in gadget chargers. Provide a handy towel rack that fits over the door to allow wet guest towels to dry. Gather a selection of favorite movies and local maps and brochures highlighting unique local sites.

styles we love

WAKE-UP CALL
Think of paint and fabric as Botox for aging furniture. A glossy coat in uplifting apple green paired with geometric bedding injects modern spirit to a traditional four-poster. Revive an old bench or seating with a bold wide-stripe fabric that repeats the bed's paint color.

OFFICE SUPPORT

above left **Don't retire vintage furnishings:** Rehire them with fresh, new uses. Here, an old secretary works as a mini home office, dresser, and bedside table. Perk up an iron bed with a linen slipcover for the headboard. Stitch or glue on stripes of grosgrain ribbon. Continue the bed's modern revival with a fresh color scheme—chocolate, gold, and blue—and graphic pillows for punch.

TASTY CHOICE

above right **Rich chocolate brown is a warm, cozy choice for bedroom walls,** promoting cocoonlike calm. Hits of bold color and graphic patterns in the rug, pillows, and lighting snap it awake. If the only spot for your bed is under a window, integrate the two with a wide valance or Roman shade and full drapery panels for balance.

Bedding buys
Don't get short-sheeted on a good night's sleep. Cotton is King Pick your best sheet material—100 percent cotton is best for softness and durability. Egyptian cotton, the highest grade, and pima cotton, a close second, have long fibers that make them notably soft and able to absorb and release moisture—a plus in summer. Comfort Adds Up Higher thread counts (the number of threads per square inch of fabric) make softer, smoother sheets. At 300 count, sheets begin to feel silky and are more durable; 600 count is considered luxury. Consider Care Percale, a cotton-polyester blend, isn't as soft as pure cotton and can pill over time, but dries faster and wrinkles less. Polyester is affordable but scratchy and stands up to repeated washings. Sateen, a cotton weave, is silky and satiny that washes like any cotton. Set the Temp Cotton flannel and jersey retain heat—good for winter. Pricey silk traps warmth, but must be dry-cleaned. Long-lasting linen is cool and grows softer with each wash.

color palette

True blue leaves a room feeling calm and composed. Keep this classic color from nodding off by using it in a playful mix anywhere in the house.

island waters, saturated, should be used sparingly and in high gloss. **Try it:** on a bench or bed frame.

glory days, an all-American hue, grounds a space. **Try it:** on a desk or porch chairs.

deep waters, a dense blue, enriches a small space. **Try it:** on walls.

dark wash, a blue-violet, accents terra-cotta or orange. **Try it:** on a bedside chair or patio porch furnishings.

stonewashed, a gray-blue hue, complements wooden and white cabinets. **Try it:** in a master bath or kitchen.

Color mastery

Learn how to decorate using this hip, hot color.

Picking favorites. When choosing a blue, consider how often you're in the room. You might tire of a vibrant blue in a living room, but find it pleasing in a cozy den or serene bedroom.

Sing the blues. A one-color dominant scheme, such as the blue bedroom here, is easy on the eyes and easy to pull off. Just vary the intensity of the color by keeping walls—whether painted or wallpapered—a few shades lighter than the bedding.

Quiet, please. Bold pattern on both walls and bed (or walls and sofa, if it's in a living room) calls for a light touch with accessories. A clear glass lamp and artwork in white frames are quietly elegant.

Stay alert. Tuck in touches of canary yellow or fuchsia—in art, accessories, and pillows—to add contrast, energy, and warmth to a cool blue bedroom.

Try this! Frame pages from a wall calendar for easy art.

EASY MATCH Blue goes with almost any wood trim or furniture piece. Try a medium blue with rich walnut, like the boxes in the night table here.

style made simple | before & after

A style-deprived bedroom could be keeping you up at night. Bare windows, stark walls, and tired bedding aren't restful. Use wallpaper, textiles, and furniture to create a look that's vivacious yet softly feminine.

BEFORE

3 common flaws

1 All white walls feel stark and unsettling.

2 Mismatched night tables don't live up to their style potential.

3 No headboard and plain bedding foster sleep deprivation.

3 fabulous fixes

1 Wallpaper on one wall becomes its own chic work of art.

2 Complementary night tables suit the room and provide storage.

3 Stylish headboard with layers of pillows and coverlets invites rest.

Try this!
Use a ceramic garden stool as a handy chairside surface for a cup of tea.

POINTS OF INTEREST
opposite **Wallpapering just one wall creates a focal point and is a budget-friendly "wow."** Bedside tables needn't match, but they should be about the same height. Here, a 32-inch-high dresser is used as a nightstand. A 30-inch-high bookshelf serves the other side of the bed. Layering an area rug under the bed adds personality.

TIGHT PALETTE
above left **Though the yellows are vibrant, repeating the same color keeps the look calm.** Similar shades of yellow, with hints of ivory and beige, unify multiple patterns in a room.

STYLE MIXER
above right **The upholstered chair and bed frame sport solid fabrics as a quiet base for patterns.** The drapery motif works because it's a smaller scale than the other patterns in the room. Mix up furniture styles, finishes, and uses for impact—such as a low black-lacquer Chinese sideboard with white wire lamps.

style made simple | before & after

Layer on stylish personality and carve out extra space despite the challenges of your room's architecture or layout.

BEFORE
3 common flaws

1 Awkward architectural slopes and spaces make the room feel disjointed.

2 The only place to position the bed is in front of a window.

3 A low ceiling makes the room feel cramped.

3 fabulous fixes

1 Quirky angles get charm with wallpaper and fabric.

2 Latticework headboard anchors the bed and allows light in.

3 Muted hues and a mix of patterns add height and airiness.

Try this!
Remake an old nightstand with paint and grass-cloth wallpaper.

DREAMY DESIGN
opposite **Abundant pattern and dreamy, muted hues of blue and taupe are everywhere. The Moroccan-style sheeting gives exotic appeal. A solid coverlet shows off its contrasting blue side when folded back.**

TUCKED IN
above left **With the addition of easy-to-arrange cubbies, a cozy chair, and wallpaper in a large-pattern floral, the orphan alcove is now a focal-point, storage-savvy library nook. A curtain panel hung from the ceiling gently cordons off the nook.**

CREATIVE CANOPY
above right **To keep the bed's placement in front of a window from screaming "mistake," a canopy was attached to the ceiling. White crown molding hides the mounting system and integrates the canopy into the room. Flowing damask panels hang at each corner, establishing the bed's importance.**

room elements | bedding

Making the bed every morning is
fun with the right bedding combo.

UP-TEMPO ARTISTIC
opposite **Skip matching bedding sets. Pick pieces that share one dominant color—the cheery green here—and one or two accent colors. Vary pattern sizes for the best mix. Top them off with artistic pillows.**

LITTLE BIT COUNTRY
top left **Crochet throws and needlepoint pillows create a patchwork of candy colors and textures perfect for a painted wood or cast-iron bed.**

MIX & MATCH
top right **Make matched bedding sets more lively. Start with two solid sheet sets (try one bright and one neutral) to mix for various looks. Top with a solid-color quilt and bold, patterned shams.**

PATTERN PLAY
middle left **Use this strategy to mix patterns: Pick a bold, tight print for the duvet; balance it with a similar yet larger print for shams; layer in striped and solid pillows and bed skirt.**

LAKESHORE SERENADE
middle right **Marine colors and patterns suit a summer sleeping space. Pom-pom trim adds playful cottage style. Try it with an upholstered headboard and bed skirt in cream.**

EXOTIC ESCAPE
bottom left **Update a dark-finish traditional bed with deep blue and fresh green bedding with exotic Middle Eastern motifs.**

CORRECT DOSAGE
bottom right **Add color for emphasis. Colors from Euro shams in a bold two-tone pattern are repeated in bolster pillows and a throw. Layer in white pieces to temper the patterns and colors.**

get organized | bedside

Say "good night" to outdated rules about nightstands. Pick the pieces that suit your needs.

Try this!
Hang a pretty serving tray in place of art.

FOR A BOOK LOVER
A tiered table borrowed from the living room makes a handsome nightstand. Use its multiple shelves as a library for journals and books.

FOR A PROP STYLIST
top left Why let creative displays happen only in your living room? Recruit a roomy console table and decorate it with objects you love. A mirror bounces light and allows a little primping space.

FOR A NATURE LOVER
top right Tree stumps sculpted into side tables cultivate an eco-chic personality in a bedroom. Shop artisan crafts shows and shops for pieces that have been kiln-dried.

FOR A TAILORED TYPE
middle left With an X-shape base, dark finish, and luggage-stitch detailing, this standing serving tray lends a modern, masculine edge to a bedroom.

FOR A NIGHT WRITER
middle right If your bedroom needs to moonlight as an office, position a small writing desk and chair next to the bed. It's handy for late-night journaling or jotting notes and lists.

FOR A FASHIONISTA
bottom left If you dream of eclectic decor, start by replacing your typical bedside table with an unexpected piece like this tea cart. The cart's bamboo styling is chic and practical, providing handy storage space for blankets and books.

FOR A RECYCLER
bottom right A repurposed computer desk makes a function-packed nightstand. Tuck away lip balm, remote controls, and other necessities on the pullout keyboard tray.

style made simple | headboards

If you're not sure where to begin a bedroom makeover, let your headboard provide a springboard for a new look.

A-PEELING ATTITUDE
above left **Furniture silhouette stickers make a graphic, fool-the-eye headboard. And they're inexpensive, low-investment stand-ins for the real deal. This peel-and-stick-on decal of an iron headboard is a great fit in a first apartment or while you're deciding whether to invest in an antique.**

SUNNY SILHOUETTE
above right **Rise and shine each morning with a shapely headboard slipcovered in a bold, energetic fabric. Made of plywood simply cut to a curvy shape and covered with foam to add cushiness, the tall headboard is perfect for read-in-bed types.**

FRAME AND FORTUNE
opposite left **Framing a large piece of fabric is an affordable way to add a luxurious focal-point headboard. Here, inexpensive decorative molding, painted and distressed, frames a piece of plywood that's been covered in cotton batting and toile fabric. The shape is echoed in a paint "frame" on the wall.**

DOOR PRIZE
opposite right **Old cabinet doors found at a salvage shop are smart stand-ins for the usual headboard. Shop for doors with a worn patina, and pick up those colors in the bedding, walls, and windows. Protect the surface with clear polyurethane, hinge doors together, then fasten to the wall or bed frame.**

Bedstead choices

The bed framework is the foundation of your bedroom—and a big investment. Choose one with a simple form for longevity. A platform bed is often low to the ground with only a headboard and no footboard, giving it a clean, uncluttered look. Four-posters were originally designed to hold hangings to insulate sleepers from drafts. Today, the soaring posts make a dramatic, room-centering style statement. Canopy or tester beds are four-posters with crossbeams connecting the posts for a romantic look. Low-post beds with finial-topped posts at their corners, a prominent headboard, and low footboards come in a variety of decorating styles. Sleigh beds recall the curves of an old-fashioned sleigh. Their substantial frames are best in roomy bedrooms. Upholstered beds have wood frames with fabric-covered headboards; some also have upholstered footboards and sides. Choose the upholstery wisely, as it will affect your color choices for the bedroom for a long time.

kids' rooms

Decorating a room that grows with a child requires clever planning, not clairvoyance. Here's how to get started.

10 Design Basics

1. PLAN AHEAD. Consider how long your child will love the bedroom style. Kids grow up quickly and change their minds even faster. **2. THINK DAY AND NIGHT.** Make sure the space is ready for daytime play and comforting at night. **3. BE FLEXIBLE.** Select elements that are right for now and can be modified easily as the child grows. **4. ASSESS NEEDS.** How many children will share the room? Does the budget allow for new furniture? Will the room include play and study space? **5. COMPROMISE.** Color, pattern, and theme choices need to suit both parents and kids. Turn the decision-making process into a fun activity for you and your child. **6. SOFTEN UP** by adding rugs to cushion hard-surface flooring, pillows to lounge against, and curtains to visually soften a room. Soft surfaces also dampen sound. **7. PICK KID-FRIENDLY FINISHES.** Opt for washable fabrics, scrubbable paint on walls and woodwork, and durable surfaces that downplay nicks and scratches. **8. CONSIDER SAFETY.** Avoid sharp edges on furniture, cords on window treatments, and furniture that tempts preschoolers to climb. Always secure heavy pieces of furniture to walls. **9. START WITH THE BED.** It's the largest piece of furniture, and it will be the focal point. **10. CLOSET SMARTS.** Outfit the closet with storage before filling the room with furniture to leave more open space for play.

styles we love

The rough-and-tumble world of kids requires durable bedroom furnishings and a get-tough attitude toward organization.

LINEAR LOOK
above left **Bold, colorful stripes on bedding and a shared nightstand with storage provide a perfect spot for two brothers. Khaki walls will wear well as the boys grow older. The headboards, made from pine doors attached to the wall using bar holder brackets and corner braces, cost less than $100 each.**

BIG WORLD VIEW
above right **A planet mobile overhead, a roller shade made from an old school map, and graphic bedding make this space kid-friendly for now and later. All it takes is a change of accessories to update for a teen. Take advantage of the slanted ceiling as a cozy spot for the bed.**

PLAYING FAVORITES
opposite left **It's only paint, right? Let a kid pick a favorite color for his or her walls. Stacks of shelves and removable adhesive give kids free rein to display their interests and collections from floor to ceiling. Tucking bunk beds into an alcove frees up floor space for play.**

TWO-TONE SUITE
opposite right **Bold colors separated by a white chair rail provide a color punch in this bedroom. The bright scheme gives a vintage spindle bed a modern look. Storage solutions—shelves, dressers, nightstands, baskets for toys—help keep kids organized and rooms tidy.**

Just for kids

Consider these kid-friendly tips. Ensure the bed is safe. Make sure the beds you choose meet American Society for Testing and Materials standards. You'll find the current standards on the U.S. Consumer Product Safety Commission's web site. Go to *cpsc.gov* and search "bunk beds." Reserve the top bunk for children older than 6. **Outfit the closet.** Equip it with hanging racks for clothing, pullout bins for large items, and storage baskets for portable small items. **Include low storage.** Shelves near the floor and toy baskets are tools you can use to teach a child to pick up after play. **Make room for imagination.** Choose furnishings that reflect your child's interests and spur creative thinking: for younger children, places to safely crawl into or to set up make-believe play spaces and arts-and-crafts tables.

SHOWSTOPPER
Alternating stripes of sky
and baby blue create the
main event: a tentlike
ceiling treatment. Green
and sherbet pink expand
the palette. While the
classic four-poster bed
style is long lasting,
freestanding furniture—
bookcase, table, and
chair—are small now but
can be replaced as the
child grows.

NOT JUST FOR KIDS

above left Furnishings and accessories need not come from the children's department. Soft colors and classic styles will keep this bedroom looking perfect for years to come. After all, kids introduce their own collections and keepsakes into the mix, so it looks age-appropriate at all times.

TURQUOISE FOR TWO

above right A favorite color grounds the scheme for a room shared by two. Use bedding as a starting point for a color palette, as it's easy to match paint to the fabric. A narrow desk with chairs for two solves a space problem. The oversize bulletin board serves both as art and organization.

Storage sleuth

What can you do with tons of kid gear and too little space? Try these ideas. Roll Out Use the space under the bed to hold hand-me-down clothing until it's ready for wear. Bed Risers These can make more space underneath; storage boxes on rollers make items easy to access. Double Duty Select furniture that offers storage space with function such as an ottoman, bookcase base with tabletop, or headboard with shelves. Wall Space A row of hooks for totes adds handy storage. Shelves can climb up a wall. Bulletin boards organize cards, posters, and art assignments. Bin It Open bins move easily and are always open for pickup time.

styles we love | learn & play

A spot dedicated to homework teaches
kids study and organizational skills under
the watchful eyes of their parents.

STUDY CENTER

**Plan a space beyond the
bedroom for kids to do
homework. Separate
built-in desks minimize
distractions. Topping a
desk with durable glass
protects the surface
while giving young artists
a place to display their
latest work. A built-in
window seat provides a
spot for parents or kids to
take a reading break.**

Try this!
Cut and fuse
felt letters
to a purchased
pillow.

TABLE FOR TWO

above left **Here's a solution for a quiet study space:** Float an island desk in the center of a room shared by two. Bookshelves provide storage space for supplies, so the desktop stays clear except during homework or art sessions.

FAMILY ZONE

above right **A bookcase/ desk center at one end of a family room lets parents supervise homework sessions and kid-time on the computer. Swivel chairs make it easy to adjust chair height as kids grow. Open shelves provide find-it- return-it storage. For the tidiest look, use baskets and boxes.**

Clutter control

Tame the clutter monster by working with your children to develop good habits. Daily: Set aside 20 minutes in the morning to walk through the house and tidy up so that everyone comes home to a welcoming space. Weekly: Devote one afternoon to set housekeeping goals for the week ahead. Put chores on your family calendar. Monthly: Go through kids' schoolwork and decide what to save, such as art or a first spelling test, in a memory box. Send a few favorites to relatives. Toss the rest. Seasonally: Donate clothing that has not been worn in a couple of seasons. Twice a year, go through toys and donate what is no longer needed.

color palette

It's no wonder pink is a favorite with the feminine set. After all, pink can be powerful or gentle and independent or a team-player. Here's how to hue it.

rose blossom, ultrafeminine and soft, makes a room glow. **Try it:** on walls.

powder blush, a nearly neutral blush pink, adds a tint of color. **Try it:** on a ceiling combined with ballet-slipper pink and white.

fiery fuchsia, deeper and bluer than the other pinks, is best as an accent. **Try it:** to paint a chair or storage box.

raspberry rouge, no shrinking pink, commands attention. **Try it:** for stenciling random flowers across a wall.

ballet-slipper pink, a muted hue, plays well with others. **Try it:** in combination with cool shades, such as turquoise, or with warm accents of wood or sisal.

Color mastery

Pinks the color of a garden of peonies signal summer freshness year-round. No wonder they're favored hues.

Try one on. Today's pinks aren't the fade-away pinks of a past generation. These pinks evoke a mood that's playful, exuberant, and comforting.

Go bold with pink. Punch up a small space such as a bed alcove with a dark pink. The richer, deeper pink shades make a space feel safe and cozy.

Partner up. Pinks can be delicate or exciting. Tans and browns wear well with hot pinks. For a fresh twist, try various shades of pink—lights and darks—with teal or robin's-egg blue.

Check light. Pink absorbs light rather than reflecting it. Observe the paint color at different times of the day and night before you commit to the hue.

Ease it in. Unsure of bold pink? Try it in accessories such as pillows or an area rug.

Try this! Cover a self-adhesive lampshade with fabric.

SWEET RETREAT A happy shade of pink surrounds a sleeping alcove with color, while a scalloped border of blue provides a sweet edge. Settle on bedding before choosing wall colors.

before & after

This over-the-garage addition takes on a starring role in family life. Once a catchall, it's now an eye-popping playroom filled with color, just-for-kids furniture, and a real stage.

BEFORE
3 common flaws

1 The room's nice bones are boring with only white everywhere.

2 An out-of-the-way space is underused and collects clutter.

3 Stained carpeting is removed to reveal plywood underneath.

AFTER
3 fabulous fixes

1 Zippy green and blue set an energetic tone for this kid-friendly zone.

2 A stage, crafts area, and study zone make it a destination worth visiting often.

3 Laminate flooring is easy to keep clean.

Try this!
Add track lighting to stand in as stage lighting.

ZONE 1—
MAKE ART
opposite **Kid-size furniture and laminate flooring ensure that the crafts area sees heavy action. A section of wall covered in blackboard paint provides an instant canvas for artists. Current works of art are attached to the walls using removable adhesive. Framing puts favorite pieces on display.**

ZONE 2—
ACT THE PART
above left **Bring on the play with a stage fit for any little actor. Grommet curtains (hung from a wire cable system) instantly create a stage, while spotlights and storage for costumes add a theatrical note. Chairs are easy to move from the crafts table for audience seating.**

ZONE 3—
READ MORE
above right **Skip the side table—a knapsack attached to the chair holds favorite books. Two chairs and an ottoman occupy a reading oasis in the center of the space. A shag rug provides floor space that's also comfy for stretching out with a favorite story.**

style made simple | bed central

TAME THE BEAST
Free up space with a multipurpose spot for sleeping, lounging, and studying. The unit is made from a captain's bed with bookcases sized for a single bed at each side. Nestling the bed along the wall allows it to function like a sofa, a perfect addition to a tween's life.

A small room has met its match: bed, dresser, and lounge in 8×10 feet.

BOX AND BIN IT
top left **End units flanking the bed provide hideaway storage that's labeled for easy use.**

DOUBLING UP
top right **Use double-decker trays to maximize drawer storage for crafts supplies. Peel-and-stick letters serve as easy-to-remove labels.**

SORT BY TYPE
middle left **Purchase sock dividers to sort and store everything from underwear to jewelry.**

UPEND IT
middle right **Turn an open cube into a file holder by flipping it on end and labeling the dividers.**

SHELVE IT
bottom left **Incorporate a handy shelf with hooks to organize clothing and showcase collections.**

CUBE IT
bottom right **Storage cubes offer multiple uses. Attach to a bookcase or hang on a wall.**

get organized | kid gear

Savvy storage for kids should be fun, creative, and easy to reach. Here's how to help it stack up.

Try this!
Add legs to a bookshelf for a bench with storage.

BOOKS PLUS
Book storage and a comfy spot for reading: What could be more perfect? An off-the-rack bookshelf set on its side pairs with a custom cushion. The cubbies are low enough for a toddler to reach.

SHELF WISE

top left **Big books, little books—a kid's room full of books. Here's a great solution: tall shelf space for the tallest books, shorter shelves for small books, and bins to hold the rest.**

ROOM TO GROW

top right **Freestanding bookcases make smart choices. There's plenty of low space when kids are small and upper shelves they can grow into. Make sure to secure tall units to the wall to prevent them from tipping.**

AHOY, MATEY

middle left **Books stay shipshape in a built-in bookshelf that puts them on display and prevents them from falling. Nautical rope threads through holes drilled in the bookshelf dividers.**

FLIP FOR STORAGE

middle right **A Murphy bed-style crafts table hooks to the cabinet when not in use and flips down to reveal crafts storage inside the cabinet. Canisters and baskets help keep everything organized.**

WILD FOR WINDOWS

bottom left **Adding a window seat with storage below is a natural for kids' bedroom storage. But including a tall bookcase and using window-style cabinet doors (use plastic for safety) creates an indoor playhouse.**

A+ FOR FUNCTION

bottom right **An organized wall-hung cabinet has space for crafts materials and doors painted to work as blackboards. Add even more function with a shelf fitted with cups to keep pens, pencils, and scissors nearby.**

WILD FRONTIER

THE
WILD FRONTIER

WILLIAM M. OSBORN

Silverstein

Where the Sidewalk Ends

HarperCollins

RINE CHRISTIAN

the Pendragon

BLE CROSS   SAM GIANCANA AND
            CHUCK GIANCANA

LARRY McMURTRY
By Sorrow's River

JOHN E.
WILLS, JR.   1688   A Global History

12,000 Inspirational Quotations   FRANK S

nch   Cooking for Kids and Cowboys

a brief history of g

fairbairn

SECTION TWO

house tours

Learn how to create a decorating
style that unites every room in
the house into one fabulous,
livable, and unique home.

modern cottage

spare style

This getaway house has the lightness and airiness of a cottage in a trimmed-back style. Clean lines and light colors keep the feel relaxed.

The clean, edited style pairs classic design with modern spareness. A limited palette of materials moves from space to space, delivering a cohesive look that delivers an expansive feel. **Double up.** Think multiuse for rooms and furniture. The dining table is also a home office. The coffee table seats four for dinner using floor cushions. The guest room is a library. **Expand space.** Use a palette of white and pale neutrals, minimal window treatments, floating furniture, and a mirrored backsplash to "grow" a house. **Give standard a twist.** Inject standard buys with decorating personality. Striped wallpaper hung horizontally, glossy white wood floors, and updated vintage pieces add originality. **Store more.** Storage units in the dining room and kitchen hold covered boxes. The coffee table's bottom shelf stores books.

OPEN ATTITUDE
One large open space includes a centered living room with a kitchen at one end and a dining room at the other. White walls and scored concrete floors unite the spaces.

modern cottage

CLUTTER KEEPER
above left **A metal bookcase keeps the cook's gear neatly arranged. Labeled boxes hold small items for cooking and entertaining.**

DINING AND WORK
left **An oval table handles dinner and office work. The metal storage unit with linen-wrapped shelves serves as a bar and provides file storage.**

SMALL AND SAVVY
above right **Open bases on the cabinetry and mirrored backsplashes add airiness to the small kitchen. The all-white palette keeps it from feeling claustrophobic.**

WELL-ORGANIZED KITCHEN
opposite **Simplicity reigns in the kitchen with white cabinets that stretch to the ceiling in one uninterrupted line. The stainless-steel stovetop, backsplash, and range hood punctuate the minimalist space.**

10 try-this simplifying tips

Learn how to copy this streamlined look in your home.

Go lean. Ruthlessly edit possessions.

Choose hues. Whites plus a few pale tones make up the sophisticated palette.

Reduce pattern. Opt for patterns in pale colors and simple designs.

Add texture. Touchable textures—chenille, linen, marble, and wood—add interest.

Plan storage. Consider bookcases with right-sized storage boxes and tables with storage on a bottom shelf.

Simplify flooring. Be consistent. This home features scored concrete on the first floor and white wood upstairs.

Mix in vintage. Find pieces at a flea market that fit the airy look but add interest, such as the chairs and stools here.

Accent gently. Bring in accessories in the palette colors, occasionally adding a focal-point piece.

Repeat. Use the same materials in kitchen and bath. Here countertops unite the rooms.

Open windows. Where possible, leave windows uncovered. Choose window treatments that disappear when opened.

MASTER RETREAT
Spare lines, glossy white floor paint, and striped wallpaper hung horizontally join forces to create a bedroom with ethereal qualities.

SPARE THE SPACE

top left **A built-in dresser makes the most of a narrow space. Drawers on one side are shallow to accommodate bathroom plumbing.**

REFLECT THIS

top middle **A counter-to-ceiling mirror expands space and reflects the mirrored door.**

BATH SPACE

far right **The shower curtain stretches to the ceiling, a trick that makes the room seem taller. A narrow chair and small garden stool add landing spots for toiletries and towels.**

STRIPE STRATEGY

bottom right **Install wallpaper horizontally so the stripes run around the room and make the space feel wider. A soothing stripe keeps a standard-height space feeling serene.**

To create a home that's spare yet interesting, choose unique colors, patterns, and objects limited to a soft, subdued palette.

open plan

modern family

This family home works within its modest footprint. Bold style covers every inch, and the open floor plan expands while providing plenty of visible storage.

When "more is more" suits your lifestyle, furnishings and a home interior with clean lines provide the perfect backdrop. **Organize the palette.** A small house looks and lives bigger with a palette that flows from room to room. Pick a few neutral wall colors; accent with stronger colors. **Maximize furniture.** A sectional provides seating space without chopping up a small room. Sliding it close to an L-shape wall of bookcases makes maximum use of floor space. **Keep it neat**. Small houses demand good storage, often open but some hidden. Open storage, such as bookcases, needs to be kept in order. Organizing by color creates stylish order. **Repeat elements.** Light wood stain and white painted finishes pair with repeating squares to deliver a cohesive look. **Embrace light**. Minimally dressed windows invite space-expanding sunlight inside. Consider blinds or roller shades that open up to hug the top of the window frame.

STORAGE ART
Books and magazines stored by spine color add an artistic touch to basic bookcases. The L-shape sofa nestles into the corner for a cozy retreat.

open plan

KID SMART

above left When it comes to storage, keep it within reach of kids. This below-window shelf provides book and toy storage.

BUSINESS CLASS

left An expanding file holder from the office-supply store organizes favorite reading material.

TRIPLE PLAY

above right A bank of three white file cabinets mimics the look of a sideboard. The shallow drawers simplify organizing paper and supplies. A set of nesting tables expands surface area when needed.

WORK NOOK

opposite A former closet, this wallpapered nook accommodates open storage and a desktop for a computer, all without squeezing the room's floor space.

10 try-this organizing tips

Making room for everything requires creativity and determination.

Plan. Create the right storage space by measuring items to be stored and match them to shelves and boxes of the right size.

Divide drawers. Use plastic, wood, or cardboard dividers to customize drawers.

Get crafty. Cover boxes with pretty papers and stack them as display and hideaway space.

Look high. Opt for bookcases that stretch to the ceiling and shelves that climb the walls.

Go low. Give kids a place they can reach so putting away toys becomes a good habit.

Hang it. Hooks keep gear organized and in sight.

Collect. Group like objects, such as globes or toys, for style and storage.

Color code. Sort objects for open storage by color for a cohesive look.

Donate. Gather items no longer needed but in good shape and give them to a local charity.

Cycle. Rotate favorite display items to reduce overcrowding surfaces.

LIBRARY WALL
A bookcase keeps stacks of reading material organized while separating the dining room from the living room. Here, too, organizing the books by color adds a design element.

SHELF KEEPERS

top left Storage adds up when shelves stack up the walls. Pegs under the bottom shelf make room for hanging items.

BOX DISPLAY

top middle Boxes hung on the wall and customized with paper liners provide a changeable display for a child.

CRAFTS CENTRAL

top right Cubes wrapped in pretty papers store small items and provide a fun contrast to the simple white file cabinets.

LIGHT DINING

bottom left Orange accents and blue-gray walls in the dining area repeat the pale-with-a-punch color scheme used throughout the house.

STACKING STORAGE

bottom right Open shelves in the kitchen add visual square footage and handy storage.

Organization starts with a careful inventory of the items to be stored. Making room for small items can have as much impact on removing clutter as adding a large storage cupboard.

order in the house

Ready to get organized? Learn how to create a place for everything in a small house, a strategy that will reward you with more living space and more style.

A well-organized home needn't be hands-off. Grouping items cleverly adds style and invites touch. **Remove bulky items.** Upper cabinets in the kitchen, heavy drapes in the living and dining rooms, and a too-big light fixture got the heave-ho. **Think slim.** Consider how a narrow bookcase or airy shelves can expand space while adding storage. **Build a neutral palette.** Warm khaki and white spread cheer around the space and provide a soft background for attractive storage options. **Rework furniture.** Consider how a chest, armoire, or trunk can be outfitted to hold gear in the style you love. **Make storage function as display.** Glass doors in cabinets create the opportunity to stack and gather pieces—dishes, glassware, books, office supplies—so they look good and are easy to find.

HOME BASE
A little floor space in the living room made room for efficient storage in a wall of bookcases. White woodwork adds a crisp note, while the blue ceiling feels like sky.

classic bungalow

FINE DINING
above left **Supplies for entertaining are kept in the dining room where they're sure to get used. A drop-leaf table in the bay window provides ample space for serving a buffet.**

LIGHT EFFECT
left **A well-placed mirror multiplies the effect of a candle collection. It creates a pretty vignette rather than just storage.**

MINI ENTRY
above right **Think of pieces of furniture as little rooms within rooms. The old pine chest serves as an entry table and bar.**

STORAGE DISPLAY
opposite **China, glassware, and linens are pretty, so show them off in a glass-front armoire. Baskets, trays, and platters keep the contents organized.**

10 try-this storage tips

Make storage stylish with these clever ideas.

Buy multiples. Purchase matching boxes, baskets, and glass canisters to use all around the house.

Tray it. Fill pretty trays with writing, makeup, or media supplies to keep tabletops organized.

Be flexible. Use adjustable shelving that's easy to change with storage needs.

Label. Keep track of contents with pretty labels.

Display it. Dress the dining room table with bowls or candles to keep clutter from landing there between meals.

Think thin. Narrow shelves fit into almost any room with ease.

Move often. Rethink how to use cabinets and desks for storage to best suit your needs.

Look up. Fill tops of cabinets with pretty objects that are used occasionally.

Use it. Recruit pretty vases or cups as storage for pencils and art supplies.

Layer. Fill a wood tote with canisters containing tableware or an olive tray with salt and pepper shakers.

IN EASY REACH
A U-shape work area provides ample counter space, while open shelves above keep the kitchen from feeling claustrophobic. Yellow paint adds cheer.

WORK ZONE

top left **Keep the laundry room neat with open shelves stacked with clutter-hiding bins.**

CORNER OFFICE

top middle **A corner of space may be all it takes to keep the entire family organized. Outfit the space with a bookcase for baskets and boxes, and add a work surface.**

BETWEEN THE LINES

far right **Opportunities are everywhere. This secretary desk is tucked in a short hall and is a storage and work multitasker.**

DETAILS COUNT

bottom right **Even the cat has its own spot thanks to a cutout in the cabinet door. Nearby bins store food and litter, while the handy sink makes cleanup easy for humans.**

Creating storage that's efficient and beautiful does much more than keep a house clutter-free. It turns collections of everyday objects into artful arrangements and makes household chores feel like creative play.

savvy remodel

the well-crafted cottage

A huge remodeling project revamped every inch of this Craftsman-style house. Learn how to use this home's smart ideas.

Turning a house with a definitive style into a home suitable for today's needs requires a plan that respects the original space and blends it with the new. **Stay neutral.** Select a palette of neutrals for wall colors and use them in every room. **Focus on storage.** Living is simpler when there's a place for everything. Built-ins do that seamlessly. **Add pattern.** Inject personality with doses of fabrics. Focus on changeable bedding, window treatments, and pillows. Use pattern to add personality and livability to rooms. **Soften the scene.** Use slipcovers to relax upholstered pieces, add rugs to cushion floors, and select worn wood surfaces to reduce worries about wear and tear. Soft surfaces also soak up sound to make a home feel restful. **Repeat for serenity.** A house feels calmer when elements, such as paint colors, fabrics, and furniture styles, flow from room to room.

savvy remodel

WELCOME HOME

above left **A covered porch and a chartreuse front door offer shelter from the weather and a warm hello. The Craftsman door sets the tone for the home's style.**

FAMILY BUSINESS

left **An office open to the master bedroom is a second adults-only space. A desk flanked by built-in cabinets provides storage for household records.**

SERENITY CENTRAL

above right **A small living room functions as a grown-up space for entertaining and doubles as a guest room. The colors here mimic those used in the rest of the house. An extra-large ottoman provides feet-up relaxation and also serves as a coffee table.**

GRAND ENTRY

opposite **Built-ins wrap the doorway between the living room and the entry. Pocket doors slide shut when the room turns into a guest bedroom. Bed linens for the sleeper sofa are stored in the ottoman, right where they're needed.**

10 try-this modern-living tips

Simple tips can keep rooms flexible to serve changing needs.

Stash in baskets. Use them to make gear mobile as you move between rooms.

Build slim. Bookcases just 12 inches deep add storage and display space to any room.

Soft storage. Purchase double-duty ottomans with soft surfaces and storage inside.

Double guest space. Trundle beds turn any child's bedroom into a guest room.

Minimize window coverings. Streamline style with frame-hugging Roman shades.

Mind the weight. Opt for lightweight furniture that's easy to move.

Hang TVs. Optimize viewing options by hanging TVs on the wall using swivel mounts.

Splurge. Include a dress-up item, such as a bit of beautiful tile, to make each room special.

Floor it. Install wood flooring in every room. Define spaces and protect high-traffic zones with area rugs.

Step outdoors. Connecting to the backyard adds fair-weather living space to a house. Consider adding a new French door.

DARK AND LIGHT

opposite **The dark mahogany furniture-look island adds a cozy feeling to the mostly white kitchen. Floors are 5-inch-wide ebony-stained oak.**

ISLAND STYLE

top left **A second sink in the island makes a perfect prep center.**

OPEN PLAN

top middle **A peninsula separates the kitchen from the dining area. The color palette and finishes unite the spaces.**

SMART SITE

top right **The below-counter microwave oven is at a handy height for school-age children.**

WORTH THE SPLURGE

bottom left **Green tiles on the backsplash add a subtle dressy note.**

TRAFFIC COP

bottom right **The island provides a buffer that diverts traffic around the cooking area.**

Kitchens today handle much more than cooking. They're designed for living with room to gather, study, entertain, and more.

KID CENTRAL

opposite **An awkward corner becomes a focal point with built-in bookshelves and a window seat in a child's room. The colorful rug and bedding bring changeable style, while neutral finishes on walls and furniture provide adaptable backgrounds.**

SUITE RETREAT

above **A built-in window seat adds a cozy seating space without decreasing floor space in the master bedroom. Doors on the lower cabinets hide bedding and a television, while open shelves showcase books.**

Inch for inch, built-in cabinetry adds more storage and more seating in less space than any other option. It's a perfect solution to make small bedrooms live big. Combining open shelves with closed cabinets and drawers expands storage possibilities.

today's farmhouse

refined rustic

Rustic plank walls, barn-style doors, and an open floor plan infuse a center-hall Colonial with a casual vibe.

The interior of the house needn't match the exterior style. But when the styles are compatible, such as the country interior in this Colonial, the feeling is more relaxed. **Stay neutral.** Mixing neutrals—from white to platinum to charcoal—keeps backgrounds flexible and noteworthy. **Play with texture.** Texture adds interest, especially in a neutral scheme. Lush velvet mingles with reclaimed wood, while shiny surfaces reflect tooled metals. Using more texture creates more interesting layers. **Go fuss-free.** Opt for fabrics and finishes that are comfortable, casual, and forgiving of spills and dings. Indoor/outdoor fabrics come in a variety of colors and textures. New versions are soft to the touch and hang in gentle folds. **Try a spare approach.** Use strong color and pattern in small doses for big effects, such as a knockout rug. Keep the backgrounds simple. **Make it personal.** An Asian dining table updated with bold orange paint is a favorite from bachelor days. Turtle prints reflect an interest in nature.

CASUAL CHIC
The living room paint color is a chameleon, changing from blue-gray to gray to green-gray. A range of other neutrals expands the color scheme. Note how the turtle prints balance the mirror in this almost symmetrical space.

THE WAY WE LIVE

today's farmhouse

HOME BASE
above left **Ceiling beams, plank walls, and a streamlined fireplace surround set the stage for this farmhouse's modern aesthetic. Furnishings—including a simple graphic rug and woodsy tables— enhance the mood.**

LIVING COLOR
above right **It makes sense to purchase expensive kitchen elements, such as cabinets, flooring, and appliances, in neutral tones and add color in changeable accessories, such as a rug and seating cushions.**

WINDOW SEATING
opposite **The breakfast room's wall of windows leaves no real wall space, so the "art" is on the floor in the form of a boldly patterned rug. A coat of orange paint updates the Asian table.**

Decorating with a modern sensibility can introduce as much warmth as any other design. Rustic woods, warm colors, and casual upholstery offer creature comforts. Streamlined shapes give modern polish.

10 try-this casual tips

Learn how to put relaxation back into your home with these easy tips.

Double up. Use two small tables rather than one big coffee table for flexibility.

Add a natural touch. Create a simple tablescape using wood bowls and something freshly cut from the garden or yard.

Go green. Use plants—big and small—to bring the outdoors into rooms.

Stack books. Piles of books, stacked on sideboards and tables, lend a casual note.

Paint. Tone down the formal and add bold color to furnishings with paint.

Try geometry. Combine circles, rectangles, and X's for modern drama.

Bare it. Leave windows uncovered to welcome sunshine and eliminate fussiness.

Step up. Gather a collection of prints of varying sizes and frame styles to charm a staircase wall.

Simplify. Eliminate mats on prints for a modern finish.

Soften. Add cushions and pillows in colors and prints to suit the season or your mood.

today's farmhouse

MODERN MIX
Classic meets modern in the entry, where a simple lamp provides a counterpoint to an intricate Asian chest.

GARDEN FRESH

top left **The neutrals-plus-color scheme works on the outdoor deck as well. Comfortable seating and put-up-your-feet tables maintain a casual family attitude.**

CLIMBING ART

top middle **Photos framed in black and gold create a collection that's revealed as you climb the stairs.**

PRINT STYLE

far right **An Asian table paired with framed turtle prints creates a perfect marriage of styles. Wall planks in three different sizes create a textured backdrop.**

SPACE SAVER

bottom right **Sliding "barn" doors are a practical and stylish solution. Here, they separate the living area from the kitchen and add a stylish accent.**

color splash

Invite the beach inside with sand-tone floors, splashes of vivid color in paint and fabric, and a strong connection to the outdoors.

Make any small home feel like it's got a big footprint and a coastline just outside the door with the best ideas from an oceanside cottage. **Go beachy.** A swath of bold aqua paint (think sky and water) and sand-color tiles (think beach) bring the seashore inside. Choose cabana stripes for slipcovers with a classic beach look. **Expand space.** Use the same floor coverings and paint colors throughout to make a small cottage live big. Opt for fewer but larger pieces of furniture. Open up the ceiling to expand visual space. **Choose a center.** Focus naturally centers on a fireplace. Put the TV there, too, and arrange furniture outward to anchor the multiuse living space. **Be playful.** Large framed prints and colorful patterned pillows add playful personality. The kicky citrus yellow and aqua blue add even more fun style. **Think outside the walls.** Create living spaces outside the house to extend the warm-weather season. Use indoor/outdoor fabrics for curtains and slipcovers, oversize tile for flooring, and candle chandeliers.

COOL CABANA
Merging kitchen, dining, and living spaces into one space is a smart strategy. By sharing style cues throughout the space, each area feels roomier. Coordinating flooring materials and colors maintains a cohesive look.

10 try-this budget tips

No one will think budget decor when you use these ideas.

Fool the budget. Try a bold paint color for style pizzazz that can cost less than $30 a gallon.

Stitch it. Buy inexpensive fabric remnants for pillows.

Cover it. Use Roman shades rather than pricey cabinet doors to disguise open shelves.

Bargain smarts. Look for furniture and light fixtures at garage sales, flea markets, and discount stores. Paint or re-cover them to suit your style.

Be artful. Purchase inexpensive posters to frame as art. Buy posters that fit off-the-rack frames.

Redo lighting. Update light fixtures with spray paint.

Check the unexpected. Shop home centers for inexpensive sisal-look rugs.

Refresh. Use bouquets of flowers and bowls of just-picked fruit for an always-fresh look.

Collect and display. Fill canister jars with pretty shells, buttons, rocks, or other found treasures.

Flirt. Add a full-length skirt to disguise a stained or weathered chair seat.

BEACH DINING
A round table is perfect for a small dining area because it doesn't restrict traffic flow. Slipcovers in a cabana stripe bring the beach inside.

SMALL BUT MIGHTY
top left **The U-shape kitchen maximizes efficiency, while the white scheme visually expands the space. The peninsula does overtime as a kitchen work center and casual dining spot.**

DETAILS COUNT
top middle **Marble countertops and an elegant faucet dress up the beach house.**

PATTERN PLAY
top right **White walls, white sofas, and a neutral rug provide plenty of space for colorful and dramatic accessories.**

OUTDOOR LIVING
bottom right **Extending the patio made it large enough for outdoor entertaining. Candle chandeliers allow for dining past sunset, while drapes provide privacy.**

fresh traditional

relative geometry

Pattern exerts an emotional pull that delivers wow power to a new house. The look is bold but not overwhelming thanks to smart use of color.

If striking but classic style is what you want, start by learning how dramatic patterns enhance the architecture of a home and brighten the space. **Create a pattern wardrobe.** Focus on shared colors to build a wardrobe of large, medium, and small patterns. Use the boldest patterns on the floor. **Build drama.** High ceilings, bold patterns, and dramatic pairings remove the ho-hum from any house. Combine strong patterns in the same colors for sophisticated interest. **Quiet down.** Use solid fabrics, pale walls, and wood flooring as a backdrop that provides visual relief from pattern. Minimize pattern to create restful retreats. **Be fearless.** Let pattern pairings evolve. Start with a few must-have patterns for rugs and window coverings. Gradually add pieces such as pillows and artwork that are easy to replace. **Mix and match.** Combine geometric patterns with free-form ones to create tempo and balance that move interest around the room. Even the base of a table adds pattern to the mix.

fresh traditional

TEXTURE PAIRINGS
above left **Texture pairs with pattern to create a livable space. Nubby fabrics, plush rugs, wicker, and glass each introduce a touchable decorating style.**

PATTERN CHOICE
left **Contrasting colors make the rug pattern bolder than the overscale but neutral prints on the chair, ottoman, and draperies.**

SCALE UP
above right **High ceilings make room for large and bold accessories such as the rectangular mirror and sconces in the living room. A bold rug serves as an anchor for the lofty space.**

ENTRY OPTIONS
opposite **A cushioned bench adds function to an entry, while accessories offer changeable pattern. Look for fun designs in pillows and throws.**

10 try-this style tips

Let shapes and patterns rule without running amok by following a few simple pointers.

Collect. Gather pattern samples before starting a project to make sure all are compatible.

Declutter. Remove the competition to let patterns take center stage.

Mix shapes. Pair curvy chairs with angular sofas.

Balance solids and prints. Use solid linens on a bed with a headboard upholstered in pattern.

Reflect. Include a mirror with a pretty shape near the entry to introduce shape and scale.

Arrange. Place large tropical leaves or a few blooms in clear glass containers to add organic shapes to tabletops.

Gather. Organize a collection, such as vintage cameras, on a single bookcase.

Stencil. Create a one-of-a-kind dresser using a stencil and paint.

Touch it. Add woven baskets or furniture for subtle pattern with natural, tactile appeal.

Go big. Use large-scale patterns on floor-to-ceiling draperies.

KITCHEN CLASS

opposite **Bold curtain panels create a focal point in the kitchen and tie this space to the open living and dining rooms. Other materials—carrara marble countertops and solid tiles laid in a diagonal basket-weave configuration—provide more subtle pattern.**

OPEN-AIR DINING

above left **Patterns play a supporting role in the dining room, letting the table settings and centerpiece shine when you're entertaining, and creating a subtle-but-interesting background when the room is not in use. The bold curtain fabric repeats in both living room and dining room, adding continuity.**

LIFE OUTDOORS

above right **In a sunny climate, this porch functions as a multipurpose outdoor room. Outdoor fabrics and weather-resistant furnishings make it as handsome as interior rooms.**

Outdoor living space that's comfortable and stylish especially makes sense in a mild, sunny climate. Indoor-outdoor fabrics and cushions stand up to sun and moisture.

PLAYFUL PATTERN
Bold patterns mix it up by reversing their light and dark backgrounds. Solid white linens provide a visual resting place.

WING REPEATS

top left **Repeating design elements, such as the wings on the chair and the bed, creates design continuity.**

SPA LIFE

top middle **A spa bath with a treetop view offers relaxation. A bold wallpaper pattern keeps it from feeling sleepy.**

SLUMBER SUITE

top right **Creamy white walls and draperies add a restful feeling to the master bedroom. French doors open to an upper-level deck.**

SLEEPING BERTHS

bottom right **In a house built for vacations, a room of bunk beds maximizes guest space. Bold curtains provide design drama and guest privacy.**

personal mix

colorful character

A home designed around family and company can be dressy and relaxed at the same time, especially when a 1950s traditional house adopts a fresh attitude.

Comfort and high style needn't be mutually exclusive with a design that gives both top priority. **Set the mood.** Pastel wall colors give this home a tranquil feeling. Mixing bold hues with pastels keeps the rooms from feeling too feminine. **Touch matters.** A variety of textures add dimension to the design. This is an effective strategy in rooms with few patterns. **Make connections.** Use color cues and furniture styles to create consistency when rooms flow one into the other. Maintaining one color palette makes the design feel cohesive and intentional. **Go eclectic.** Create a collected-over-time look by pulling furnishings from more than one decade. Mix antiques with contemporary art and family heirlooms with new purchases. **Light right.** Lights can improve a room significantly. Use dimmers for overhead lighting. Consider floor lamps for flexibility and sconces for a touch of drama.

PETAL FRESH
Peony pink freshens
the living room walls.
Bold pops of color are
introduced in pillows and
accessories that can be
changed with ease.

INDIA

CAROLINA HERRERA

personal mix

FINE DINING
above left **The mirrored cabinet at one end of the breakfast room serves as elegant storage for book bags. Using a sisal rug adds a casual texture to the sophisticated space.**

KITCHEN STYLE
left **Calcutta gold marble, a glass tile backsplash, and a beaded chandelier add dressy notes to the white kitchen.**

OFFICE PERKS
above right **Bright and bold choices define this office-in-a-corner. Hot pink paint on the vintage desk balances the sunshine yellow trellis wallpaper. The chair continues the playful attitude.**

ART SHOW
opposite **A modern painting hangs above a French settee at one end of the breakfast room. This mix-and-match strategy is at play throughout the house.**

10 try-this classic tips

Give traditional style a fresh new look with these easy ideas.

Be bold. Mix in bright, invigorating colors—such as sunshine yellow—to keep stodginess at bay.

Reflect. Mirrors on tabletops and cabinet doors add elegance and a bit of a surprise.

Collect. Don't hesitate to let antiques and modern art share space on the same walls.

Contrast. Arrange fancy French chairs on a sisal rug or hang a chandelier in the kitchen for a splash of freshness.

Tint it. Soft pastels add just the right amount of color on walls.

Surprise. Paint a vintage piece of furniture an eye-popping shade.

Master the mix. Balance objects using classic symmetry and pieces, but mix up the objects' pedigrees.

Add removable pattern. Layer it on with pillows, throws, and artwork.

Raise windows. Hang curtains just below the ceiling to make rooms feel elegantly taller.

Land softly. Opt for cushions and pillows with sink-in down filling to make even the most formal sofa inviting.

CLASSIC COMBO
A formal demilune table,
perfectly balanced with
almost-matching lamps,
contrasts with the wood
dining chair. The
flowering tree branch
pattern was hand-painted
on the paneled walls.

CORNER OFFICE
top left **A sweet vintage desk offers a perfect spot for writing notes in the master bedroom.**

COLOR POP
top middle **Floor-to-ceiling built-in storage hides clutter in the family room, while a window seat with a fluffy pink cushion adds seating.**

OPEN HOUSE
top right **Flowing spaces require consistency of color, such as the dark hardwood flooring that connects these rooms. Gray walls in the entry ground all the soft colors.**

LIGHT LAYERS
bottom left **An elegant chandelier accents the height of the ceiling in the master bedroom. New French doors open to the backyard.**

WINDOW DRESSING
bottom right **Window treatments in the guest bedroom rev up the color scheme by mixing kiwi with pink.**

Maintaining a comfortable, not-too-cluttered style requires constant editing. Take time to regularly remove excess items so the pieces left in place will be noteworthy.

artistic cottage

the gallery house

Bright colors, bold patterns, and clever storage give this rustic house a personal style.

Casual living and an artistic flair are graceful style companions in a home's interior design. **Unify surfaces.** Bamboo flooring that sweeps through all the rooms and rough-board walls keep the look cohesive. Neutral walls also maintain the look. **Layer color and pattern.** Pretty fabric combinations create focal points with an artistic attitude. Consider bold stripes on furniture, accented with colorful patterned pillows and throws. **Float furniture.** It's a smart way to define territory in a small house without moving walls. Anchor furniture groupings with rugs. **Reduce, reuse, recycle.** Pair eco-friendly finds with reclaimed wood and vintage textiles and furniture that add character and don't require new manufacturing. Plus, collections give a house personality. **Organize with style.** Tuck storage space under eaves, repurpose vintage cabinets to hide clutter, and turn fun finds into clever storage.

DISPLAY CENTRAL
above **A narrow console table works hard for flexible storage and display space. Tucked behind the sofa, the table's display mixes with artwork on the wall.**

CASUAL DINING
opposite **Walls clad in rough-cut lumber and washed in white paint add a rustic note to the dining area. Wicker chairs with wood legs add to the rustic appeal.**

artistic cottage

CORNER UTILITY

above left **Windows** replace upper cabinets in the corner kitchen. A nearby pantry provides plenty of hideaway space for cooking gear.

SITTING PRETTY

left **Oval platters hung in graduated sizes subtly decorate the wall. Wallpaper adds quiet pattern and repeats the green used throughout the cottage.

STAIR STYLE

above right **A pretty striped rug carries the home's color palette to the upper level.

OPEN OFFICE

opposite **Old framed shutters open up to show off a handy bulletin board made from peel-and-stick cork sheeting. Look for shutters still in their frames at a salvage shop and paint them to match your decor.

10 try-this artsy tips

Learn how to add an artist's touch to any small home.

Connect with color. Cool blues and greens lend a calm attitude and let art pieces stand out.

Play with paint. Stencil a pretty pattern on a wall for personal style.

Repurpose to organize. Turn framed shutters into a bulletin board or a tackle box into a card file.

Reflect. Expand space and light with old French-door frames backed with mirrors.

Call on curtains. Use them as a low-cost option for hiding storage cubbies.

Frame it. Create art by framing a scrap of fabric, a pretty card, or a family photo.

Have an "ungallery" space. A room with little on display, such as the kitchen here, gives the eye a place to rest.

Show off. Cluster glass floats in a bowl or pretty votives on a tray. Collections create focal points.

Light the night. Use good lighting in every room to enjoy the artwork all day.

Be creative. Turn a colorful step stool into a bedside table.

MIRROR IMAGE
Under-eave storage space can create order in an attic bedroom. Open cubbies hold baskets, boxes, and stacks of books. Use shutters to close off some areas.

NESTING SPACE

top left **Make the bedroom as personal as you please. A pretty stencil on a rustic wood wall takes the place of a headboard. Layered textiles dress the bed with color and pattern.**

MINI LAUNDRY

top middle **Curtains magically cover up hardworking spaces such as the under-stair laundry. Use grommets to make curtains easy to slide.**

UNDER-EAVE CLOSET

top right **Tuck hanging space for shirts under the enclosed attic eaves.**

TUB TERRIFIC

bottom left **A claw-foot tub romances the bathroom. Look for vintage tubs at a salvage store.**

TABLE FOR ONE

bottom right **A calming view and a pretty collection of accessories can turn any table into a place to linger.**

A small house filled with graphic patterns and bright pops of color provides the perfect place to display artistic treasures.

scandinavian modern

nature house

Homeowner architects doubled the size of their home while infusing it with Scandinavian sensibility. The result is family-friendly and tied to the great outdoors.

Even when you choose a singular style, options for expression abound. Consider what's most important to you, and the style will adapt. **Connect outdoors.** For these homeowners, a connection to the outdoors and the woods beyond was the top priority. The design includes banks of windows and a screen porch surrounded by trees. **Create double-duty rooms.** Lightweight furniture is easier to move for games on the floor. Slipcovers provide easy-wash options when the living room is also the family room. **Warm with color and pattern.** Pair brightly colored patterned rugs and fabrics with white walls for a look that's cozy and clean. Experiment with bold textile designs. **Mind the inches.** Plan the details in compact rooms to maximize living and storage space. **Keep it cozy.** Original smaller rooms in older homes offer a workable scale of living. Remodeling to improve connections between rooms expands the view so small rooms feel larger.

scandinavian modern

BRIGHT IDEA

above left **Sunshine spills into the kitchen and down the hallway through large windows that wrap around the walls. Blond woods and white walls reflect the light deep into the house.**

STYLE ADDITION

left **The original house (painted white) has a new, red addition designed with a top-level master suite, a ground-floor kitchen, and a lower-level playroom/guest room.**

LIGHT DINING

above right **A light-filled nook in the kitchen is the home's only indoor eating spot. A window-backed cabinet holds a collection of colorful glass.**

SPARE EFFICIENCY

opposite **The efficient kitchen includes a bank of cabinets on one side and an island on the other. Wood cabinets and flooring add visual warmth.**

10 try-this family style tips

Learn how to create a home that makes everyone feel comfortable.

Pile on the pillows. Combine solids and patterns for design flexibility.

Go round. Eliminate hard edges with a round coffee table and curved corners on other tables.

Display. Put objects of importance on top of a stack of books.

Clip it. Use drapery ring clips to make it easy to slide curtain panels that softly slouch for a casual look.

Build a library. Add floor-to-ceiling bookshelves to house a family collection of books.

Stash away. Gather baskets to make attractive storage and tote space for kid gear.

Soften floors. Add rugs to create comfort and to break up all-wood flooring.

Light it up. Use lamps near reading spots, pendants for task lighting, and recessed lighting in work areas.

Post it. Create spots for display using bulletin and magnetic boards.

Simplify. Employing a single color palette throughout a house focuses design choices.

SUNNY BATH

top left **One long towel bar stretches from the shower to the sink area for maximum efficiency.**

FRAME ART

top middle **A framed magazine cover is from a 1930s issue featuring the original 1,200-square-foot home. An 1,100-square-foot addition meets the practical needs of a modern family of four.**

ART INSPIRATION

far right **A bulletin board covers one wall of the office and keeps favorite artwork on display. The home's color scheme reflects the ebullient tones of the children's paintings.**

PORCH PERFECTION

bottom right **White paint modernizes the screen porch. During mild weather, the porch becomes an outdoor dining space.**

Family-friendly spaces offer areas for comfortable lounging, rooms devoted to learning, and color that inspires an artistic life.

workroom

Our hands-on decorating guide offers
real-life advice, savvy insider tricks,
style lessons, product tips,
quick projects, and more.

get started

Designing rooms should be fun—not fraught with worry. Breathe deep, take your time, and let us coach you through our steps for planning a perfect room.

10 steps to creating a plan

1. SEEK INSPIRATION by tearing pages from magazines and catalogs; print images from websites; consider what attracts you to favorite objects, destinations, even restaurants. **2. REVIEW WHAT YOU HAVE** to work with in the space, from furniture to fixtures. Ask yourself: What should I remove, recycle, or repurpose in my design? **3. DRAW A FLOOR PLAN,** photograph walls straight on for future reference, and jot down all window measurements. **4. DECIDE WHAT MOOD** or look you want the room to project and how you will use the room. Now's the time to plan for storage and organization. **5. DECIDE WHICH COLOR** will dominate on the walls, floor, and ceiling. Consider where patterns, colors, and finishes might appear in fabrics and on furniture. Think about accent colors. **6. START A BUDGET SPREADSHEET.** Cushion it with 20 percent for unexpected repairs or delivery fees. **7. GO ON A FACT-FINDING MISSION.** Shop around, sleuthing in stores and online for products and prices. **8. WEED, PRUNE, AND PARE DOWN** your ideas and selections. Transfer these ideas to a board with floor and wall plans. Step back and review. Then create your master design plan. **9. RECRUIT YOUR DREAM TEAM.** Line up installers and repair professionals. **10. SET THE SCHEDULE.** Take into account delivery lead times and allow for possible delays.

tips we love | getting going

Learn how designers start a project.

"Take your time. Live in a new house for at least 6 months before making decorating decisions."

—**Janna A Lufkin,** interior designer

"File favorite magazine pages and downloaded images you love. Include rooms, wall colors, shapes of upholstered furniture (ignore the fabric and concentrate on the form), fabrics (ignore how they're used), curtain styles, lamps and lighting, flooring, and rugs. You'll discover trends that will define your favorite look or room style."

—**Elaine Griffin,** interior designer

"Map out furniture on the floor in painter's tape to ensure the pieces will work in the room. Painter's tape removes easily when you're done."

—**Grant K. Gibson,** interior designer

"Look in your closet for clues about the colors, patterns, and silhouettes—simple, tailored, or fussy—you are most comfortable living with. Chances are if you love colorful, ruffly clothes, you'll be comfortable with colorful, ruffled furniture."

—**John Loecke,** interior design

"Collect design magazines and books from all over the world, old and new."

—**Annette Joseph,** interior designer

lessons

THANK YOU

HAPPY BIRTHDAY

Thank You

Understand basic terms about the color wheel to have more confidence choosing hues.

1 primary colors
Red, blue, and yellow are the primary hues. These colors are pure; all other colors are created from primaries.

2 secondary colors
Orange, green, and violet are secondary hues, equal parts of two primary colors combined. Yellow plus blue yields the secondary hue green.

3 tertiary colors
Mixing a primary color with the secondary color next to it creates a tertiary color. Each blend results in a less vivid hue. Yellow and green blend to make apple green.

4 neutrals
Think of these "uncolors"— beiges, browns, grays, black, and white—as the supporting players, pairing nicely with most hues and providing great backdrops. Brown and beige range in intensity from soft latte to deep cocoa. Dark neutrals, including rich pewter gray, calm other colors and add sophistication. White enlivens colors, while black strengthens and stabilizes.

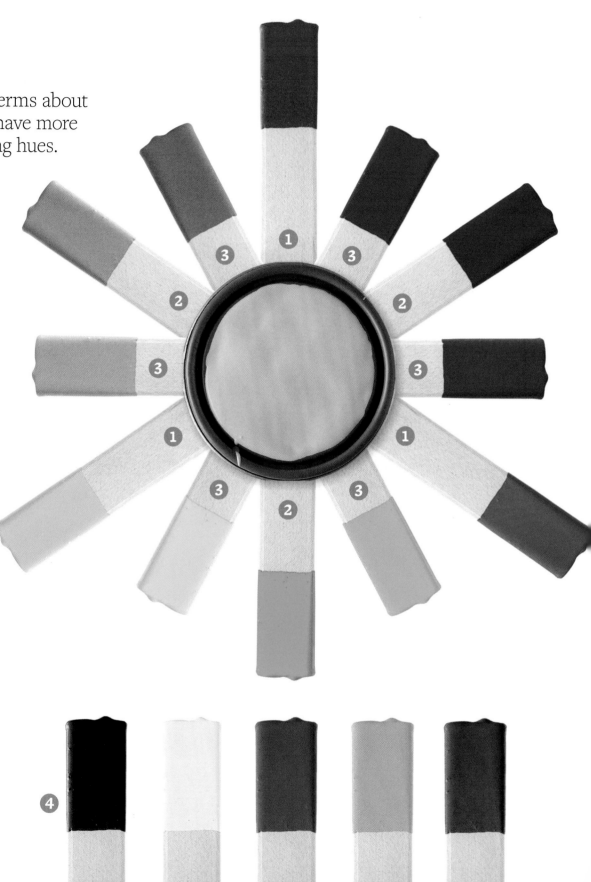

Steer the color wheel toward a fresh look for your rooms.

Set a mood. Warm, active colors—yellow, orange, and red—energize a space. Use them to heat up a north-facing room or fuel appetite in a dining area. Cool, passive colors—blue, green, and purple—calm a space, making them perfect for a bedroom. Let one color dominate, then include opposite colors and neutrals, but avoid all-warm or all-cool palettes.

Create contrast and balance.
Complementary palettes—such as fuchsia and apple green—use colors directly opposite each other on the color wheel. Create balance by pairing colors of the same value, or intensity. Let one color be the star, and provide visual resting spots with neutrals.

Use thy neighbors. Analogous palettes—such as yellow-green to blue—are made from colors side by side on the color wheel. Because these colors are closely related, they are easy to use together and create a relaxing environment. Use a favorite color as the main hue and add two neighboring hues. For a livelier look, vary the intensities of the neighboring colors.

1 ENERGY POLICY
Wake up a room with a warm/active color palette. This breakfast area's vibrant orange seating gets an added boost from its color complement—a soft icy blue—in pillows and tilework.

2 SOFT AND SERENE A cool/passive color scheme of soft blues works well in a bedroom. Emotional responses to blue and its association with water, sky, and air may lower the pulse rate, creating calm and serenity.

3 SIDE BY SIDE Use analogous colors that sit next to each on the color wheel for a harmonious look, as in this room's yellow-green, yellow, and yellow-orange trio. Clean, bright white accents match the intensity of the colors and give eyes a place to rest. Aqua glassware supplies contrast.

4 EQUAL FOOTING
Pick complementary colors with the same intensity, as in this dining room with eye-catching blue seats and bold orange draperies. Ground the space with dark woods, neutral accessories, and metallic finishes.

Five crowd-pleasing color combinations.

1 ONE COLOR + WHITE Use different shades of a color—here it's blue—to easily pull together a room. Add crisp white—in fabric, trims, furniture, and millwork—as a unifier. Add interest by varying textures and patterns.

2 CHOCOLATE + MUSTARD + CREAM Play up the silhouettes of furnishings and architecture with deeply saturated chocolate brown walls. Add high contrast with cream trim and furnishings. Then add a third color with brown undertones, such as the mustard here. Brown is best in rooms with lots of natural light.

3 NEUTRALS + NATURE Defy expectations of a neutral color palette: Stick to browns, silvery blue-grays, and creams, but vary patterns and textures. Use pale wood paneling and play up the graining against glossy white furniture and metallic accessories.

4 LEMONGRASS + PEONY Indulge your creative side with colors that tweak tradition. Try a tart, lemony upgrade of khaki—the linen upholstery here. The peony of the floor tiles and pillows is a deeper, not-too-sweet take on pink that grounds the space. Go neutral for the background—sandy walls and simple shades.

White done right
Use this universal color wisely.

Seek a match. Compare swatches of whites before you commit.

Play glossy against matte. Use high-gloss white paint on wood furniture and trim, and chalky matte on walls.

Mask architectural quirks. White unifies uneven walls, windows, and trim. Use it to play up the curves and shape of a table or chair.

Avoid "super whites." These "builder-grade" whites can be cold and glaring on walls. Try warmer off-whites tinged with undertones of honey. Or sync white walls and trim to the color undertones of the room's furnishings—for example, add a tinge of blue to white in a room with blue fabrics or accents.

Create a blank canvas. Choosing white for floors, walls, and furniture allows accessories to easily change with the seasons or design trends.

Try white porch paint for indoor floors. Avoid entryways; upkeep gets easier the farther you are from the front door, such as in a bedroom.

Try this!
Test colors in a room without a paintbrush— look under "Tools" for the latest color-envisioning tool on *bhg.com*.

5 BLUE + YELLOW
A perennial favorite. Choose blues and yellows with similar intensities, such as the blue bedding and yellow wallpaper here. Keep the look fresh with bold floral and striped patterns; add texture with a modern woven headboard. White in the patterns and sheets unifies the look, makes colors appear brighter, and gives eyes a resting area.

Learn how to wow with the power of pattern.

Start basic. Consider the 60/30/10 approach. Use 60 percent of a favorite pattern, 30 percent of a second pattern, and 10 percent of a third as an accent. Try three patterns in a range of scales, such as a narrow stripe, a midsize geometric, and a bold floral. Include solids in supporting roles on a sofa or floor.

Repeat power. Repeating colors from pattern to pattern can help even disparate patterns seem like first cousins. Accentuate underplayed shared colors in the patterns. If you use one pattern, such as a stripe, repeat it somewhere else in the room, even if the color and scale change.

Play pattern matcher. A large-scale print can be too big for a pillow or small room, and a complicated pattern might disappear in the folds of drapery. Not sure? Bring home fabric, wallpaper, rug, and curtain samples to test the look. A neutral ground, the solid background color on which a pattern is printed, or solids pull colorful patterns together to create visual interest without taxing a space with too much of a good thing.

1 GO BIG Select the largest patterns first. A neutral patterned rug sets the scene, while striped chairs layer on pattern with color. Touches of pattern appear in accessories and artwork throughout the room.

2 BE BOLD Try combining patterns you love, such as this collection of a modern floral, two stripes, and a row of framed prints.

3 FOLLOW THE NUMBERS Explore the 60/30/10 approach when you dress your bed— 60 percent striped sheets and cases, 30 percent black and white geometric shams, and 10 percent solid kiwi.

4 SOFTEN UP Add pillows as a low-cost way to explore your pattern personality. Copy colors from the most colorful pillow.

Start a pattern palette by pinning favorites to a style board.

5 SPOTLIGHT THE SUBTLE Coordinate patterns by matching less prominent colors, such as the blue-gray in the floral pillow here that's repeated as a blue-gray print on the seat cushion.

Think like a decorator

Here's how decorators use patterns to change perceptions.

Create a focal point. Patterned curtains naturally call attention to windows, while a bold geometric on a single wall can create architectural interest in a boxy space.

Change attitude. Use gingham fabric to relax a formal chair, a geometric wallpaper to update a vintage cabinet, or a colorful toile on a sleek sofa.

Reshape space. Wide horizontal stripes shorten tall ceilings, while vertical stripes raise the roof. A bold pattern in strong colors can square up a long, narrow room.

Set the style. Consider favorite patterns such as ikat, paisley, toile, or damask. No other element creates a decorating style for a room as easily.

Reflect the seasons. Use bold or deep colors to warm up a room for winter, and use light, airy prints for a summery look.

lessons | scale, rhythm, balance

Scale, rhythm, and balance are a hardworking design trio. Here's how they create a sense of harmony.

Play with scale. Scale refers to visual size—how objects look next to each other and how they fit in a room. Varying the scale is key to creating interest. Rooms need a mix of big, little, tall, and low things. Obvious choices—small objects in a small room—may not always work.

Get design rhythm. Rhythm—the way colors, patterns, and shapes fill a room—keeps a space interesting because it requires constant eye movement. The tempo can be lively and playful with bold color and pattern or slow and graceful with soft color and texture.

Put balance to work. Balance works on the teeter-totter principle. If a large seating group at one end of a room lacks a counterweight—built-ins, an armoire, or a weighty painting—the room seems lopsided. It's not necessary to match a chunky sofa pound for pound. A grouping of a rug, a few chairs, or a table can match the visual weight of a sofa.

1 FORMAL SYMMETRY Use this to create mirror-image balance in a space. Objects match or are close enough in size, shape, and color to look like they match. Symmetry is soothing to the eye. A little asymmetry—the objects in the painting and items on the cabinet—keeps the setting interesting.

2 DOMINANT ITEM A large piece of art adds dramatic scale to the room and balances the visual weight of the table. Unexpected pairings, such as the standard-size chandelier over the large table, add interest.

3 EVEN COLOR REPETITION Pops of strong yellow in a neutral space create rhythm that keeps the eye moving around the room. Repeating fabric patterns, touches of orange, and fringed throws also energize the design.

4 ALL IN PLAY Scale. Rhythm. Balance. They're all present in this arrangement. Scale is reflected in the contrasting size of the objects. Rhythm shows up in repeating colors, materials, and themes. The arrangement of objects on both sides of the large print shows asymmetrical balance at work.

Practice the design lessons of scale, rhythm, and balance by creating arrangements on a tabletop or shelf.

1 ASYMMETRY Evenly distributing visual weight without creating a mirror image is asymmetrical balance. Here, two large pieces of art are balanced with a large white expanse and anchored by a bookcase that's filled in on one side to balance the art above.

2 CENTRAL POINT A large hanging pendant delivers playful scale above the game table. Chairs around the table illustrate the concept of radial balance. Even if objects are not perfect matches like these chairs, they can still balance if they are similar in shape.

3 MULTIPLES CREATE MASS Six framed photographs provide the scale of a headboard without the bulk. They also create rhythm that increases visual interest.

4 RANDOM COLOR Scatter a dominant hue, such as orange, throughout a room. Color repetition keeps the eye moving and weaves the space together. Bold colors rev up the energy, while shaded colors calm it down for balance.

5 GROUP FOR INTEREST Clustering small objects, such as books and photographs, creates one big impact with scale. Small objects that are scattered around a room can be overlooked.

Think like a decorator

Experiment with tricks the pros know to gain design confidence.

Rearrange a room. Get the feel for using these design elements by creating different but balanced arrangements of pictures, books, and lamps on the tables flanking a sofa or bed.

Add weight. Increase the visual weight of a too-small dining chair with a slipcover. Need a preview? Drape fabric over the chair.

Group dynamics. Two small tables provide symmetry and create the weight of one large coffee table.

Surprise subtly. Look for objects that barely break symmetry, such as three of one thing.

Go big with less space. A large headboard delivers a grand focal point and requires only 4 inches of depth.

Use contrast. In a neutral color scheme, for example, choose hues that range from dark brown to pale ivory to add rhythm.

Add texture for tactile warmth and visual appeal.

Let opposites attract. For design interest, pair smooth and rough, sleek and nubby, shiny and matte. Layer a shaggy rug on a smooth floor, fill a silver compote with pinecones, or add metal upholstery nails to a velvet chair. Textures can steer a room toward the feeling you want—feminine, rustic, or glamorous. They can also alter the visual temperature from warm to cool. Choose nubby textures for a soothing attitude and lots of shine for a high-energy design.

Star or supporting cast? Texture works both ways. A stone fireplace can be the star of a room while a handful of stones in a ceramic dish add subtle texture. Toss a fur throw on the bed for winter to instantly alter a room's mood. Rough plaster walls provide visual support for modern metal chairs.

Repeat the feeling. Textures need repetition. Consider using wicker baskets in a space with a wicker chair. Combine leather on a chair and a leather magazine holder. Repeat the stone on the fireplace facing in a backsplash.

1 BEYOND THE OBVIOUS Color and pattern often upstage texture until you take a closer look. The silky lampshade provides contrast to the rattan chair. Stacks of books, a curvy tray, and a wool throw on the ottoman show the subtlety of mixing textures.

2 TOUCH EQUALS WARMTH Textures such as wool curtains, woven blinds, and a sisal rug relax the formal attitude of the furniture in this dining room, making it warm and welcoming.

3 REPEAT FOR EMPHASIS Using similar textures multiple times adds polish to a room. The stone wall picks up the texture and tone of the vintage stone sink below it. Note that the refined mirror provides wonderful contrast to the rough stone.

4 ENCOURAGE EXPLORATION Shiny textures, such as the cabinet handles and the leather on the ottoman, also can be rough. Placing these textures close to seating puts them within touch, a good way to let people experience the contrast.

Vary textures—from shiny silver to nubby wool to rough wood—for visual and tactile interest.

5 LAYERS OF INTEREST
Experiment with texture combinations by creating collections such as stones in a ceramic bowl, sisal rug samples on a silver tray, or twine wrapped around embossed paper.

Think like a decorator
Learn how to feel the difference texture creates.

Take note of texture. Every surface and element in a room has texture. Be aware of how they interact to make a space interesting. The same material can be rough or smooth, such as a finely woven wool throw and a knitted wool throw.

Support texture with color. Rustic textures play well with deep colors and neutrals. If you use a bold color, such as hot pink, partner it with a refined texture, such as glass, honed marble, or velvet.

Signal function. High-thread-count linens and silk are suited to the delicate nature of a bedroom. Nubby fabrics and sisal rugs stand up to activities common to a family room.

Put texture within reach. Color and pattern can produce dramatic effects from afar, but texture demands a closer look. A well-designed room issues an invitation to touch.

tips we love | use of color

Foolproof ways designers choose, use, and love color in their rooms.

EDITOR'S FAVORITE
Follow the rule of three. When you pick a color, use it at least three times in a room.

"Buy an artist's canvas and paint it with your color choice. Hang it on the wall and watch the color as the light changes. You can try several canvases to narrow down your alternatives."

—**Mark Woodman,** color specialist

"For small, dark spaces, I prefer anything but white. There's no truth that white makes small spaces look larger. It makes you notice how small they really are. Rather, I prefer color, and the darker the colors the better the walls visually melt."

—**John Loecke,** interior designer

"Pick colors using objects as your guide—an old celadon teapot, the burnt sienna in a paisley fabric, a blade of grass, favorite candles."

—**Sasha Emerson,** interior designer

"Choose a colorful or patterned lamp shade. Suddenly your room seems more alive and vibrant."

—**Janna A. Lufkin,** interior designer

surfaces

Explore paint—the No. 1 makeover product.

Be adventurous. Paint is relatively inexpensive; if you do the labor, it's possible to change a room or a piece of furniture for less than $50. So instead of reaching for a safe neutral, branch out into color. Try mixing sheens such as a glossy ceiling and matte walls. Experiment with paint techniques such as stenciling. Brush or spray-paint a variety of surfaces, including wood and metal.

Create a palette of paint colors. Gather paint chips of your favorite colors and take them with you whenever you shop for other paint colors. A wardrobe of colors that works together is a great way to create a cohesive decorating style throughout your house.

Consider new products. The paint industry has revolutionized many of its products in the past few years. These better-than-ever paints are eco-friendly, super durable, self-priming, and available in a range of finishes and formulations appropriate for everything from laminate countertops to concrete floors to fabric. Learn the latest about new products by visiting paint manufacturers' websites.

1 CONCRETE Let your creativity loose on a concrete floor. Porch and floor enamels with urethane-modified alkyd resin or acrylic latex opaque concrete stains handle foot traffic. Use painter's tape to create a striped pattern like this. And outline the pattern with a band of solid color to create a "rug."

2 METAL Spray paint suitable for metal surfaces gives a dated light fixture a fresh, colorful attitude. Disconnect the light fixture before painting, mask the electrical parts, and take the fixture outdoors to paint.

3 FABRIC Look for paints formulated for use on fabrics to ensure that a project like these painted curtains can be washed or dry-cleaned. Most fabric paints work on natural and synthetic fibers and are nontoxic, permanent, and water-soluble until dry.

4 DRYWALL OR PLASTER Paint may be a wall's best friend, but consider turning the freshen-up treatment into a style statement. All it takes is a happy hue, like this bold pink, and a generous dose of white. Painting only a portion of the wall makes bold colors less overwhelming.

Paint lets you express your decorating style while you flex your do-it-yourself skills.

5 WOOD Revive a dated dresser using paint formulated for wood. Make the project green with a no-VOC primer, top with one coat of paint, and sand paint off the corners to mimic age.

Think like a decorator
Get smart when using paint.

Mix it your way. Love a color that's too strong for walls? Ask the paint store to mix in just half or less of the pigment. Or add a little white paint to soften a too-bright hue, black paint to gray the hue, or a complementary color to dial back the brightness.

Shine on. Experiment with sheen as a design tool. Consider dark gloss paint for drama, matte sheen against semigloss to differentiate trim from walls, and metallic glazes or paints to add a little glimmer.

Reuse and recycle. Designers have a collection of never-fail paint colors they return to time and again. You can, too, if you jot down favorite paint hues in a decorating notebook.

Master illusion. Use paint to expand the perceived size of almost anything. Paint a small dresser a bright hue and it will "grow" in size. Paint a ceiling a light blue and it will appear to be higher.

Bring out your inner artist with five favorite paint projects. The simplest? Paint a woebegone piece of furniture a happy color.

1 BOOKCASE Refresh a dated bookcase with semigloss paint made for wood. Use primer, especially over oil-base paint. Mask off the back of the bookcase, and roll on a bright color.

2 HEADBOARD Add pattern and color with no artistic ability required. A headboard shape cut from medium-density fiberboard (MDF) provides the perfect surface for paint. Pick a bold hue for the background. Choose a large-scale stencil, white paint, and a roller to add pattern.

3 SISAL RUG Select a simple pattern for best results. Use painter's tape and a straightedge to create the pattern. Paint squares using interior semigloss paint. Dip a flat trimming brush into the paint; pounce the brush vertically to cover each section. Work paint into the texture and along the painter's tape edges.

4 FURNITURE Buy an old piece of furniture for its shape. Prep is crucial when starting with a vintage piece. Wash first with a wood-safe cleaner. Make repairs to the structure and the surface. Protect with two coats of primer. Pull out that favorite too-bold hue for this project—a touch of bright color energizes a room. Spray paints make quick work of the project.

ECO-FRIENDLY PAINT

Want to go greener with your paint choices? The key is to look for low-odor, no-VOC paints. They're good for your home and the Earth because they use water-base, rather than petroleum-base, solvents.

5 LINEN-LOOK WALL
Add character to drywall using a linen-look technique. You can buy the needed products packed in a kit along with instructions. Prep the wall with white semigloss paint. Divide the wall into vertical panels using masking tape. Working with a partner, roll glaze over the surface, then drag a canvas brush through the glaze both horizontally and vertically. Remove one strip of tape and continue spreading the texture to the next section.

Paint like a pro
These tips help create perfect surfaces.

Test. Paint large samples on foam-core boards. Check the color at various times of the day to ensure you've found the right shade.

Prime. It guarantees the new paint will stick. Match primer to the surface, including plastic or metal. Tinting primer to the top-coat color adds depth to the project.

Select sheen. You've got choices: flat, eggshell, semigloss, or high-gloss paints. Gloss finishes reflect light, while flat paints disguise wall imperfections. Consider matte paints that are safe to scrub for areas of high use.

Brush right. Check the paintbrush label to make sure it's suitable for your paint product.

Fight dampness. When painting a bathroom or basement, use moisture-resistant paint that inhibits mold and mildew.

Finish. Remove painter's tape (per the manufacturer's instructions) to prevent tape from bonding to the surface or paint. If the paint has dried along the tape, run a crafts knife gently along the tape edge; slowly pull away.

Get hung up on wallpaper's transformative magic.

Be prepared. Wallpaper adheres to most clean, dry surfaces free of mildew, grease, and loose paint. Sand away bumps and use wall filler to repair any imperfections. For badly damaged walls, use a lining paper. Apply wallpaper primer/sealer tinted to the paper's background color to hide any gaps between strips.

Know your numbers. A single "American" roll covers 36 square feet. A single "European" roll covers 25 square feet. Most wallpaper is sold by the double roll (twice the amount of length). A paper with a large repeating pattern may require extra paper.

Pick your paper. Match your paper to your budget, lifestyle, and DIY skills. Vinyl-base wallpapers are the least expensive, most durable, and easiest to apply and remove. Nonwoven vinyl- and VOC-free papers are breathable and less prone to mold and mildew. Papers labeled "scrubbable" endure frequent cleaning, good for an active home. "Washable" papers should only be wiped with a damp sponge. "Strippable" wallpaper easily pulls off the wall in one piece.

1 BOOKSHELF If you've never wallpapered, start small, such as lining the back of a display case or bookshelf. This project provides impactful color and pattern and plays up the shapes of displayed objects.

2 DRESSER Use small doses of wallpaper for big impact. Rejuvenate a tired dresser by papering its drawer fronts. (For a coordinated look, paint its body to match a hue in the paper.) Use a small scrap of paper to perk up a worn lampshade. Wrap and staple small pieces around art canvases for instant art.

3 ENTRYWAY It's OK to be bold in a small space, especially in a transition zone, such as a foyer. A "busy" all-over pattern like this damask, when selected in a darker color, grounds the area. Limit pattern or choose solid colors, such as this dark chest, to allow the pattern to delightfully dominate the space.

4 KITCHEN Dress up a kitchen with wallpaper. Tie wallpaper colors to those in the surfaces or dishware. Though bold, the pattern here doesn't overwhelm a galley kitchen because it's used on end walls only.

Try this!
For a handy wallpaper calculator with helpful installation tips, go to *bhg.com* and search "wallpaper basics."

5 ACCENT WALLS

Wallpapering just one wall works wonders in a room, becoming a mural-size work of art. If using a striped paper, choose stripes that are medium scale with only slight variations in color. Go narrow, and the stripes will seem like they are vibrating; too wide and they could look like a circus tent.

Think like a decorator
Use wallpaper to solve style challenges.

Change ceiling heights. Visually raise a low ceiling by putting a vertically striped pattern on the walls. Lower a high ceiling to make the space feel more intimate with a rich, dark paper with a tighter pattern, such as a damask or paisley.

Add architecture. Embossed vinyl-coated papers give the look of beaded-board paneling and are paintable, too.

Lend natural texture. Grass cloth, made from woven grass fibers, offers touchable, neutral texture that's earthy and sophisticated. Pair grass cloth with glossy painted furnishings for dramatic contrast.

Go for temporary touches. Try peel-and-stick, repositionable wall appliqués in geometric shapes, motifs, and murals if you want a dose of pattern and color (perfect for a kid's play area) without the commitment or effort.

Get glamorous. Today's fashion-forward papers include metallic inks and embedded glass beads for sparkle. Try them in smaller spaces such as a powder room, dressing room, or bedroom.

Learn the what, where, and how of selecting fabric.

Start with the room's key fabric. It establishes the color scheme, mood, and function. First, decide how and where it will be placed. Will it be the foundation for the room and used for curtains or upholstery, or is it a focal-point fabric perfect for a few pillows? For neutral fabric, consider how other fabrics with texture or color will expand the palette. If all the fabrics are neutrals, add contrast with dark and light tones and interesting textures.

Think upholstery. Consider wear and tear before choosing upholstery fabric. In general, the sofa fabric needs to be the toughest in a family room. A solid or slightly textured fabric will give you a lot of flexibility to change the room's look with accessories later.

Accent for style. Select accent fabrics to move the color palette around the room. Accent fabrics need not be as hardworking as upholstery fabrics, but they do need to offer style. Use them for small, replaceable pieces such as pillows, throws, and lampshades.

1 SLIPCOVERS Slipcover in lightweight chintz, linen, or cotton. For hardwearing upholstery, use fabric woven from a combination of fibers, including synthetics. Fabric grades do not indicate durability.

2 LAMPSHADES Wrap a drum lampshade in fabric for a smart finish and an unexpected look. Look for customizable self-adhesive lampshades to make this project easier. Match the pattern repeat to the shade's height.

3 FURNITURE Make a big change with 1 yard of fabric. Slip it behind glass doors on a cabinet for a bold pop of color.

4 EMBELLISHMENTS Expand your fabric's style with tassels, cloth tapes, and other striking embellishments. Use one of these options along the top or bottom edge of curtains, around the bottom edge of a lampshade, or around the perimeter of a pillow. Choose an embellishment that picks up a color in the fabric to blend in, or one that contrasts with fabric to stand out.

5 CURTAINS For curtains that drape in gentle folds, use medium- to lightweight fabrics such as chintz, cotton, flannel, linen, silk, and taffeta. Think beyond the window: Use curtains to surround a bed, divide a room, or replace plain closet doors.

Think like a decorator

These strategies employ fabric to toss in style and comfort.

Make a mood. A boxy room looks luxurious with silk drapes and a velvet ottoman, or playful with patterned cotton curtains and colorful pillows.

Soften the outlook. Relax rooms with curtains and tablecloths, upholstery, and pillows. Fabrics also absorb sound, so they're perfect for noisy spaces.

Ease the care. Opt for soil- and stain-resistant fabrics to withstand the onslaught of children and pets. Indoor/outdoor fabrics guarantee durability and deliver good looks and a soft finish.

Suit the season. Wool traps heat and feels warm in winter. Light linens and cotton reflect sunlight, promote evaporation, and feel cool in summer.

Instantly warm your home with the comfort of wood.

Consider the options. Wood can be sophisticated and elegant, earthy and natural, or modern and pure. Each wood introduces color, pattern, and texture. Well-known species, such as oak, walnut, and maple, have gentle graining, making them interesting without overwhelming a room. Exotic woods, including zebrawood, wenge, and koa, have stronger colors and grain definition that make a bolder statement.

Try wood anywhere. Consider incorporating wood in a room beyond great casegoods. For example, planks can surface walls, ceilings, and floors. Molding accents window and door surrounds, baseboards, and ceiling trim.

Play to the finish. An adaptable material, wood with a simple finish of penetrating oil shows its natural color and grain. Stains deepen or even completely change the color of a wood. Reclaimed wood reflects the conditions of its original use to create a rustic feel.

1 DECORATIVE ACCENTS Add touches to layer on warmth and interest to rooms: Use affordable, off-the-rack millwork, trim, and even finials for lamps and curtain rods. Explore the many shapes, grains, and color choices of wood at your local home center.

2 WORKING PANELS One-side finished plywood in 4×8-foot sheets provides an affordable wall finish that gives a space warm golden tones, a natural grain pattern, and an unexpected modern spirit. Use a clear-coat finish for protection that doesn't alter the color.

3 SIMPLE SHELVING A touch of wood instantly warms any space. Here, three maple shelves stack up the dark-paneled wall to add style and storage. Alternatively, combine wood species and wall surfaces with similar tones for a subtle effect.

4 WEATHERED PLANKS Salvaged wood adds rustic character to walls and ceilings. Repurposing salvaged wood is an Earth-friendly option. Check local salvage yards and Habitat for Humanity's ReStores for reclaimed wood.

Wood is a highly flexible material. Consider the variety of colors, textures, and forms that can add interest to your rooms.

5 BOARD-AND-BATTEN Cedar boards topped with thin wood strips have been used in American homes since the 1800s. Achieve the same effect by nailing thin vertical wood strips over drywall. Paint unites the materials.

Think like a decorator

Harness the power of wood as a decorating material.

Expand space. In a small home, run the same wood flooring or wood wainscoting from room to room as a unifier.

Let it star or just shine. One wood-paneled wall can be the star of a room. Cover every wall with wood, however, and the star fades into a fabulous background.

Set the mood. Solo or in combination, wood changes the mood of a space. Weathered beams mixed with car siding offer a casual look. Beaded-board paneling creates an instant cottage look. Exotic wood bookcases deliver a modern vibe.

Add instant character. Crown molding highlights the ceiling, while deep baseboards change the proportions of a room. Balusters and a newel turn a staircase into a focal point. Carved pieces, such as brackets, medallions, and moldings, add decorative details on cabinetry and doors.

surfaces | stone & tile

In love with stone and tile? Bring them happily home.

Control the cost. Stone and tile offer a stunning variety of beautiful colors, patterns, and textures. All of that can come at a hefty price per square foot, except for very basic tile. Make the purchase worth the expense by using stone and tile as a focal point in any room. That might mean a stone fireplace in a family room, an expanse of granite countertops in the kitchen, or a shower paved in marble tiles.

Manage the negatives. Stone and tile floors are cold underfoot, slippery when wet, and conducive to noise. Conquer the problems with smart solutions: Use radiant heating panels under stone floors, mosaic floor tiles to reduce slipping, and rugs, curtains, and upholstery to dampen noise.

Be creative. The range of stone and tile products offers the opportunity to create your very own look. Mix varieties of stone in a bathroom or kitchen, combine tiles in patterns and colors to create one-of-a-kind wainscoting in an entry, or refresh a vintage dining table with a tapestry of tile attached to the top.

1 FOCAL POINT Options in tile and stone offer variety from classic to modern. Just a few well-chosen pieces used as a backsplash, inset in a table, or wrapped around a mirror will create a statement.

2 BATH Bubbly circle tiles add a playful attitude behind the tub. Mosaic tiles come on mesh-backed 1-foot-square sections for faster and easier installation.

3 HEARTH WALL Stacked stone instantly faces a fireplace wall with character, texture, and color. Fireplaces start with focal-point status and are further enhanced with a tile or stone facing.

4 FLOOR Brick-shape tile in dirt-hiding tan with gray grout makes a forgiving floor for an entry, kitchen, or bathroom. Texture in the tile and regular grout lines increase slip resistance when wet.

Think like a decorator
Begin with these solid materials and an engaged imagination.

Start with a grand plan. Stone and tile can be expensive, so use them where they justify the expense. Consider a countertop-to-ceiling wall behind a cooktop, an entry floor, or a fireplace wall.

Go custom. Tile comes in pieces that can combine in endless options. So get creative when planning a custom tile installation. Map out several combinations using graph paper.

Use more rather than less for drama. On walls, use more tile than drywall to make a statement. When the tile reaches higher, it feels richer and looks more finished. Consider laying tile all the way to the ceiling in a shower.

Work with the sheen. Use glossy stone and tile on vertical surfaces where daily use won't dull them; embrace the reflections that lighten a room. Opt for matte finishes for floors and counters. A matte finish makes stone and tile colors look deeper and is less affected by daily wear and tear.

Sturdy as stone is, the surface is often porous. Use a good sealer to prevent staining. The same is true for grout.

5 KITCHENS Granite remains one of the most popular countertop materials. It provides good looks with easy care. This kitchen offers proof that granite plays well with other materials: The wall tiles are glass.

tips we love | making rooms livable

Designers share the simple ways they make rooms cozy without sacrificing style or budget.

"Comfort is surrounding yourself with special things. I love to collect things in a room. This separates a merely decorated room from a fantastic one."

—Annette Joseph, interior designer

"Beautifully finished drapes or shades are to a room what a great handbag is to someone's day-to-day dressing: You can certainly function without them, but once you have them, you wonder how you lived without."

—Patrice Cowan Bevans, interior designer

"Get that expensive-pillow squish from any bargain pillow cover when you swap the foam for a down insert."

—Michael Walters, stylist

"A tray on the table in your foyer to drop your keys and mail in, with space to park your tote bag, too."

—Elaine Griffin, interior designer

try this

try this | wall art

If living room walls could talk, what would yours say? Put some personality in your living space with five solutions for above-the-sofa art arrangements.

1 COLLECTIVE DISPLAY Think outside the frame for art ideas. A vase displayed on a wall bracket pairs with plates to become art in this salon-style arrangement. Botanical motifs and color unite the pieces. Here, the grouping's lower edge is 8 inches above the sofa, the most prominent piece is at eye level in the center, and the display's borders reach just beyond the sofa's arms.

2 A STEP UP Symmetry creates a striking focal point. Hanging the varying-size frames in an ascending arrangement introduces motion. To plot placement, determine the space needed, then line up frames along the baseline and use a level to mark the positions.

3 ON THE GRID To guarantee pleasing balance, hang art in gridded, uniformly spaced rows. Use sets of frames and mats in the same size, style, shape, and color.

4 SOLO STAR Mount a bold fabric print such as this black-and-white dandelion design on oversize fabric stretchers from an art-supply store to create a bold, gallery-like art piece.

Easy art installation
How to hang wired frames accurately.

Hold the art to the desired height; mark the top of the frame on the wall with painter's tape. Measure the art's width and sofa's length; use those dimensions to mark where the left and right sides of the piece will be. Adjust the tape marking the top of the art to the center of this measure so the nail will be centered.

Hold the wire up (*above*) and use a tape measure to determine the distance from the stretched wire to the top of the frame.

Go back to the wall and measure down from the top of the painter's tape. Mark this spot—it's where you'll pound the nail.

Hammer in the nail and hang the art, using a level to ensure evenness. Remove the painter's tape.

5 GROUP DYNAMICS
Visualize a grouping of art or objects with paper stand-ins. Trace outlines of the pieces on kraft paper, label them, and cut out. Use painter's tape to try arrangements on the wall. Install picture-hanging hardware through the paper, then pull the paper away and hang the art.

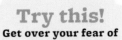

Try this!
Get over your fear of poking holes in walls. Key "how to hang pictures" into the search bar at *bhg.com* for helpful advice.

try this | wall art

Empty walls but plenty of artwork? Here's help with the most vexing and common problems when it comes to displaying your treasures.

1 DISPLAY CASE Sneak a peek of art inside a bookcase with books and objects, or on a cabinet top for a pop of color, pattern, or whimsy.

2 LINE UP Use artwork to create architectural character. Hang a series of framed art—same subject matter—shoulder to shoulder in a continuous line and at a height to suggest crown molding. The technique brings a cozy feeling to tall-ceiling rooms. Try the same technique at chair-rail height.

3 IN ROTATION A proud parent can display a child's ever-changing artwork without resorting to the refrigerator front. Create a constant canvas from a section of plywood wrapped in burlap. Attach art to the canvas. Swap the art often. To add depth, use frames of varying thicknesses and frame risers.

4 WINDOW WORKS Rooms with lots of windows and little wall space can accommodate art. Lean and layer framed works on the floor beside an armchair for a relaxed look that recalls an artist's garret. Also try this technique along a wide hallway or on a bedside table.

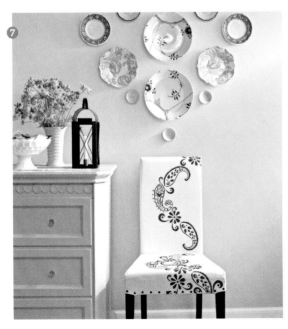

5 AFFORDABLE ART
Vintage magazine covers make eye-catching art. Match the content of the covers to the room—such as this lineup of cooking magazine covers on a kitchen wall. Unify the covers by using matching frames and colored mats. Shop flea markets for collectible magazines.

6 RISING INTEREST
Turn a staircase wall into an art gallery. For graphic impact, unify the grouping by using all-black frames and black-and-white images. Try vintage photographs or illustrations from vintage books. Start with a small group and add over time.

7 STANDOUT STYLE
If paintings and photos aren't appealing to you, hang shallow objects, such as this cluster of ceramic plates, to give walls dimension. Pick pieces with a unifying color or pattern. Start by hanging a trio of similar plates vertically, then radiate out, hanging pairs symmetrically.

8 CONVERSATION PIECES
Entice visitors to sit and relax by hanging art behind a table and chair. Positioning art lower on the wall, starting just above the tabletop, draws attention to the space, and the area feels more approachable.

Hang together: Bring generations of your family together for a reunion—as framed art displayed throughout your home.

1 ON A LEDGE Display an ever-increasing and changing supply of family photos on picture ledges that let you lean, layer, and replace framed images as new favorites are snapped or discovered. For a sophisticated display, paint frames a single neutral color such as white to unify the look.

2 SHELVE IT Bookcases are prime real estate for a photo gallery. To soften the case's lines, attach photos directly to the bookcase using adhesive strips. Stand smaller photos on top of neat piles of books. Large frames with large mats will showcase smaller photos beautifully.

3 FAMILY TREE Adhere a large decal of a tree in a vivid color (decals made from signmaker's vinyl remove easily without damaging walls). Decorate it with framed family snapshots. Shop for large decals at online emerging artists' websites such as *etsy.com* or *shopscad.com*.

4 CHILD'S PLAY Meaningful mementos— a child's drawing, a favorite greeting card, a starfish—give a wall of photos the personal flavor of a scrapbook. Mount family snapshots in neutral frames. Group pictures 2 to 3 inches apart in a random pattern.

5 DESK TOPPER Color snapshots hold together as an arrangement when placed in coordinated frames. Different shapes, sizes, and styles look unified as long as their overall color or finish is similar. Stack the frames on books or small easels.

6 OPENING ACTS Use mats for graphic oomph in photo displays. Play with the shape, placement, and number of openings in the mats, and vary the width of borders. Print photos in black and white and sepia tone. Use black frames with mattes in two tones—white for simplicity, green for a shot of color.

7 PERFECT UNION Unify a collection of old and new images—and give vintage portraits a modern feel—with matching frames in one bold hue. Vary heights and frame sizes for a casual feel. Pick up the color of the frames with a few accessories.

8 BACK STORY Choose an unexpected spot, such as the back of a door, for a quartet of small favorite photos, each in a unique frame. Position the largest print at eye level, then hang the rest above and below in a vertical line. For a secure, no-wobble attachment, use hook-and-loop fasteners.

try this | storage

For every storage woe there's a clever resolution. Consider how these ideas might lead to your own storage answers.

1 UPSTAIRS, DOWNSTAIRS

Overflow from upstairs? Maximize wall space in a basement room with a wall-hung storage unit. Keep items organized and dust-free in covered, labeled containers. Line the bonus space under the bottom shelf with metal trays to keep messy boots in order.

2 GOING MOBILE

Put your office or hobby supplies in one place—on a rolling storage rack. Casters make it easy to move to wherever you want to work. Use baskets to organize the contents on the shelves. This unit is handsome enough to hang around all the time.

3 UNDER COVER

Turn study plywood shelves or a prebuilt bookcase into a pretty console that adds style to the living room. A skirt slips over the top of the unit and conceals baskets for shoes, boots, hats, and camera equipment. The glass top protects the fabric.

4 SEW PERFECT

Organize sewing supplies in one accessible spot. The vintage secretary offers show-off storage plus drawers and doors. Open shelves organize boxes, bowls, and glass containers. Keeping items in view and labeled makes them easier to find.

10 to try now

Storage ideas that start with supplies you have on hand.

Stack fine china using paper plate dividers.

Keep a shoe cleaning kit near shoe storage.

Use luggage tags as labels for baskets.

Turn a toast rack into mail slots.

Scent a linen closet with an open box of soap bars.

Add casters to a covered metal bin to hold dog food.

Stack oversize books as a side table.

Store plastic garbage bags in the bottom of the trash can.

Line drawers with wallpaper scraps.

Add magnets to the inside of the door of a metal medicine cabinet to hang jewelry.

5 CRAFTASTIC
Organize craft supplies with ventilated shelving sized to fit storage boxes and bins. Fabric scraps and loose papers stay under wraps in canvas boxes, while colorful art supplies are on display in clear containers. Adjustable shelving can be reconfigured as needed.

Pick the best ready-to-assemble closet system for your reach-in closet. Tailor it to your clothes storage style, whether you are a folder, a hanger, or a shoe lover.

CLOSET PERSONALITY:
the folder

Install as many shelves as you can squeeze in, plus a small amount of hanging space for both long and short clothes. Shop for epoxy-coated steel systems with ventilated shelves that hang off vertical tracks and can be adjusted easily. They also promote ventilation around clothes to reduce the possibility of mold, mildew, and pests. Size matters. Shelves should be about 12 inches deep, roughly the depth of a stack of clothes, eliminating wasted space in front or behind. Group like with like. Pair jeans with jeans, for instance, because same-size items stack more neatly. Don't stack higher than about a foot, and leave at least 6 inches between the top of the stack and the next shelf for easy reaching in. Center your attention. Put clothes you wear most in the center at eye level. Add drawers to collect smaller items. If you don't have drawers, use a basket or two. Position them below eye level so it's easy to peer in.

CLOSET PERSONALITY:

the hanger

Max out horizontal rod inches by dedicating two-thirds of the closet to hanging short items. Invest in flocked hangers so clothing stays put. Shop for epoxy-coated steel systems with multiple rods for hanging and with shelves in veneer or melamine. For the double-hang area, put the shortest clothes on the top rod and hang the bottom one as high as possible under them. Use space freed up near the floor for a shoe rack or storage bins. Organize garments by category and separate with labeled hanging tags. The more specific the categories, the better. For example, subdivide your shirts into short- and long-sleeve, or casual and dressy. Organize by color within a category. Keep shoes, purses, and jewelry in hanging organizers. This way you can see them alongside your clothes. Use specialized hangers to maximize storage. Hang up to six skirts in the space usually reserved for one by using a folding skirt hanger. Shop for similar specialized organizers for accessories such as purses.

CLOSET PERSONALITY:

the shoe lover

If you adore shoes, put them front and center in cubbies. Plan enough cubbies to house every pair you wear in season. Shop for a laminate system (they come in white, cherry, or maple) with shoe cubbies, drawers, and shelves. You'll get the look of a high-end custom wood closet on a do-it-yourself budget. Store slim shoes, like flats and flip-flops, two to a cubby. Use spare slots for belts, scarves, and clutches. Keep off-season or special-occasion shoes on the top shelf, in clear pullout boxes or their original cardboard. Tack a photo of the pair to the front of the box. Drawers give the closet a polished, built-in look; add handy closed-door storage for folded clothes. Bulky items such as sweaters and purses can go on the open shelves. Eke out another sliver of storage by using the shelf below the top row of hanging clothes. It's best for things that fold up small, like tights, T shirts, or socks.

try this | organization

The right storage in the right spot can add style as well as organization. We've gathered ideas you can use whether you're starting from scratch or adding on.

1 UTILITY CENTRAL
Build a work zone using pegboard, a workbench, and storage. Paint the pegboard in bold stripes. Add panels stitched from outdoor fabric to hide clutter. Wire strung through eye hooks on the front edge of the cabinet holds curtain clips that allow panels to slide easily. Add organizing features such as a magnetic spice can organizer, bins, and a twine holder.

2 FAMILY ORGANIZER
Assign each family member a hanging basket mounted on hooks beside an entry door. Add painted letters to identify each basket's owner. A fabric liner adds color and pattern.

3 ART POCKET
Use a canvas belt for gardening tools to organize art supplies where they're used. Attach adhesive-back hook-and-loop tape to the table and the belt and mesh the two together. Pockets hold pens and paints.

4 DROP ZONE
Doors closed, it's a buffet. Open, it's the super-efficient nerve center of a busy family complete with charging station, resupply drawers, and mail slots. Drop-front lids on plastic bins contain school papers, while magnetic bars on the doors hold important notes. Labels keep order.

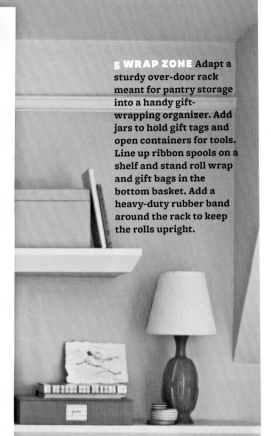

5 WRAP ZONE Adapt a sturdy over-door rack meant for pantry storage into a handy gift-wrapping organizer. Add jars to hold gift tags and open containers for tools. Line up ribbon spools on a shelf and stand roll wrap and gift bags in the bottom basket. Add a heavy-duty rubber band around the rack to keep the rolls upright.

10 to try now
Think quickly and get organized.

Install small metal knobs on the side of a sink base cabinet to hold kitchen towels.

String up a curtain rod and use ring clips to display children's art.

Store wrapping paper upright in a laundry basket. Loop twine between handles to hold rolls of ribbon.

Slip sheet sets inside a pillowcase so they're easy to keep together.

Paint a child's dresser with colorful chalkboard paint. Write the drawer's contents in chalk on the front.

Turn a vintage bucket into a magazine holder.

Store ribbon rolls on a paper towel dispenser.

Display game pieces inside glass canisters where they're handy to find and artful all the time.

Glue decorative paper to a metal baking sheet for a fun magnet board.

Spray-paint mailboxes, one for each family member, to hang by the back door as personal message centers and clutter catchers.

Busy, right? You'll love these simple accessorizing projects because you can make them in a snap—perfect when you find a just a smidge of time to decorate.

1 SHADOW ART Frame a jewelry collection in a shadow box. Use pushpins to secure the jewelry to foam-core board cut to fit the back. Stack three shadow boxes up the wall for stylish dressing room art.

2 CITRUS PRESERVES Fill glass containers with lemons, limes, and oranges. The fruit stays fresh for a week or more, and the display will lift everyone's spirits immediately.

3 WALKING BOUQUET Think of home while you're out for a walk and collect a few sprigs of this and that from roadside ditches and woodland acres. Display your finds in simple containers.

4 ON THE SIDE Line a basket with a metal cooking pan to create the perfect landing zone for often-used cooking supplies next to the stovetop.

5 DOUBLE VISION
Hang a mirror to double the blooms on a tabletop display. After hanging the mirror, add a ribbon sling as a colorful accent. (The decorative sling won't support the mirror.)

10 to try now
Simple touches add a little beauty.

Wrap ribbon bands around vases and votive candleholders (but not the candles).

Tie and knot a large scarf around a pillow for a quick makeover.

Replace knobs on a dresser for a style lift.

Place a scented bouquet of herbs in the kitchen.

Lean framed art against the wall instead of hanging it.

Leave curtains unhemmed so they puddle on the floor.

Use an occasional chair as an easel for a framed photograph.

Create mood lighting by plugging lamps into an extension cord with a dimmer.

Prop a platter behind the kitchen sink as an instant backsplash.

Slip a plastic or glass container inside a vintage tin for a one-of-a-kind vase.

try this | projects

Turn everything from dishware to wallpaper into an expression of your style—using items from the crafts store, grocery store, home center, and flea market.

1 SPLASH HAPPY Turn a trio of towels into a colorful tablecloth that's durable and washable. Join the bath towels with wide rickrack that's sewn or glued in place. Use hand towels as oversize napkins.

2 GLAM DROPS Take one standard chandelier, add old and new chandelier drops in a vivid array of colors, and stand back and bask in the glow. If you can't find colorful drops, brush translucent glass paint on clear drops and beads.

3 SCRAP ART Turn leftover pieces of wallpaper into art for your home. Look for inexpensive poster frames to frame the paper. Use wallpaper adhesive to glue the paper to the frame backing. You'll have about an hour to reposition the paper before the glue dries.

4 DOTTY DESK Turn flea market dishes into an inspiring set of desk organizers. Use a porcelain paint pen to repeat a simple circle pattern on each dish. Follow the use and care instructions on the pen.

5 DRESSER REDUX
Take the boring out of an old dresser by covering the front with an oversize poster cut to fit. Prime the dresser, remove drawers, then adhere the artwork to the dresser frame using spray adhesive. After the glue dries, trim the paper along all edges. Spray drawers with adhesive and apply the artwork; trim edges. New knobs finish the project.

10 to try now

Make time for a few crafts projects.

Unify flea market frames using crafts paint in a range of pastels.

Line the inside of a lampshade with vibrant wallpaper.

Stencil an artist's canvas for changeable wall art.

Make a mini screen by cutting a bifold closet-door panel in half and covering it with fabric.

Hang clipboards on the wall as "frames" for art.

Apply chalkboard paint on the inside of a cabinet door for an instant message center.

Hang a curtain rod and curtain behind the bed as an instant headboard.

Cut a map into frame-size pieces, frame, and hang together on a wall.

Make a duvet cover from two sheets sewn together; add ties along the open top edge.

Make a no-sew dressing-table skirt: Use the hemmed end of a purchased curtain. Cut to length plus 1 inch to turn under on the top edge. Attach using upholstery tacks.

Paint, paper, and fabric are at the heart of decorating projects. They offer color, texture, pattern, and possibilities. Use them in a room makeover.

1 PILLOW POPS

Try this solution for plain pillows: Cut designs from solid-color fabric (these are dishtowels). Adhere the designs to iron-on fusible webbing, then fuse the designs to the pillow tops. Slip aluminum foil inside the pillow fabric layers when fusing the design to the pillowcase.

2 SPLATTER PANELS

Try this fun technique on a nonpermanent surface, such as art board. Use a speckling brush available at art stores; randomly drip paint splotches. Cut the art board to size to fit in the back of a bookcase; use double-stick tape to hold it in place.

3 SCRAP ART Turn

paper and fabric scraps into art. Unite the frames with one color. Place the frames on the floor to try different arrangements. Cut foam-core board for the frame backing, if needed, and glue or tape fabric or paper in the frames.

4 PATTERN HEADBOARD Cover the

front and sides of medium-density fiberboard (MDF) with wallpaper to create a unique headboard. These panels measure 20×84 inches, but other size panels are available. Secure panels to the wall at the top edge.

5 CLIMB THE WALL A graphic flower stencil climbs the dresser front and continues right up the wall. To stretch a stencil for a project like this, repeat the middle of the stencil several times and stencil the top of the pattern last. Using one color plus white keeps the look fresh.

10 to try now
Create fun accents for your home.

Replace a bathroom towel bar with a tidy row of three to five hooks.

Buy a book of black-and-white photography to cut up and frame.

Paint a curtain finial and install as a supersize hook for a work bag.

Personalize a lampshade with paper letters from the crafts store. Use adhesive dots to secure the letters to the shade.

Install a scrap of pretty paper on the inside panel of a cabinet door.

Purchase vinyl-coated fabric to skirt a plain pedestal sink or to cover a picnic table.

Color a metal light fixture by covering the electrical parts and spray painting.

Use exterior paint to add a stencil design to a pillow made from indoor/outdoor fabric.

Make a window shade by folding and taping the top edge of a sheet of decorative paper over a tension rod.

Create a hurricane lantern by nesting a small glass cylinder inside a larger one. Fill the area between the cylinders with sea glass.

tips we love | simple joys

These little luxuries and standby solutions bring great joy to our designers and their homes.

"Walls painted with flat paint— it's almost chalky on a wall and makes a room seem softer."

—**Grant K. Gibson,** interior designer

"I can't give up in-floor outlets. They give me the freedom to pull furniture away from walls and arrange a room any way I wish without having lamp cords visible."

—**John Loecke,** interior designer

"Colorful throws in cashmere or wool make a space seem inviting. It's always a luxury for someone to be able to use a throw and be warmed by it."

—**Annette Joseph,** interior designer

"I rely on simple canvas bins and bushel baskets to hold everything from firewood to laundry."

—**Janna A. Lufkin,** interior designer

"I can't give up scented candles in every room, lit almost daily; lavishly thick bath towels that I score on sale online; and, best of all, pressed bed linens."

—**Elaine Griffin,** interior designer

EDITOR'S FAVORITE
Collections of old glass, white bowls, and coffee table books. Displaying your collections on shelves is a great and easy way to achieve a polished look.

know-how

Pull together a stylish, layered wardrobe for your windows.
Pick a favorite look, then shop for its key pieces.

EASY, BREEZY COTTAGE Start with **flat drapery panels** in a relaxed, ticking-stripe fabric in faded or muted colors. Hang from a **bamboo rod and rings** for natural texture. Add a base layer—a **flat-folding shade** made of a natural woven material—hung inside or on the window frame.

URBAN COTTAGE Select a **simple panel** in a textured fabric such as linen in a fresh, eco-chic color. For a modern attitude, construct the panel with a broad band of a corresponding color at the top. Hang from a **dark-metal rod**; add a **roller shade** in a natural weave for privacy.

FREE SPIRIT Pick **full, simple panels** in a sharp geometric or graphic floral with large metallic grommets. Hang from a clean, brushed-metal rod with cylinder-shape finials. Forgo a base layer when using a bold pattern.

EASTERN INFLUENCE Look for **semisheer cotton or linen panels** in an exotic, ethnic print—a Moroccan ikat or an Indian paisley, for example. Pair with a **sheer, sun-filtering roller shade** in a linen weave and hang from a dark-bronze rod with a shapely modern finial.

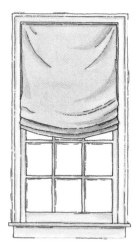

CLEAN AND SIMPLE A relaxed **Roman shade** mounted inside the window frame discreetly plays up a window's trim, keeping attention on the architecture. Its soft, swag hemline adds casually elegant shape. Choose hefty heathered linen for texture and visual weight.

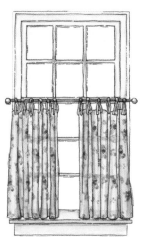

CAFÉ CULTURE Hang **café curtains** from a café rod along a window's bottom sash to allow light and views up top, privacy and prettiness below. Pick a smaller-scale print to avoid overpowering a small window.

CASUAL ROMANCE
Shop for plain panels with flirty dressmaker details like ruffled edges or dress up a pair of plain panels with ruffles you make yourself. Fold a 6-inch-wide piece of fabric in half, then press flat. Pinch fabric every inch or so (*above*), and stitch it to the underside of the panel.

Try this!
Before you buy a window covering, see how it may look in your home by using the Try-a-Window Treatment tool at *bhg.com*.

Retail solutions
Adapt off-the-rack window coverings for a perfect fit.

Add inches. Use clip hooks rather than rod pockets to hang curtains and gain a few inches of desired length.

Pump up the volume. Sew two panels together side by side to create extra fullness.

Border lines. Purchase an extra panel in a contrasting color or pattern to cut and stitch to tops or bottoms of panels for added length.

Inside job. Cut an extra panel lengthwise and attach the two parts to the inner edges of your panels for added width. A contrasting color adds a crisp outline.

Fake it. Make a designer-look roller shade with a fusible-fabric shade kit (sold at sewing centers) and a yard or two of your favorite fabric.

Get personal. Personalize plain panels by gluing or stitching on ribbon or trim, or stenciling on a graphic border or overall design using fabric paint.

know-how | window wardrobes

Don't let misfit windows put a wrinkle in your decor. These attractive solutions address the top five troublesome window shapes.

1 SKINNY WINDOWS ON A LONG WALL
Fatten up windows by hanging an extra-long curtain rod that extends well beyond the window edges, then push your panels to the edges of the window frame. For the illusion of height, mount the rod close to the ceiling.

2 ARCHED TRANSOM ABOVE A WINDOW
Keep the semicircle bare to emphasize its shape and maximize natural light. Hang a rod and drapery panels where the arch top and window meet to make tall-ceiling rooms feel cozier, less cavernous.

3 PLAIN SLIDING DOORS Mount blinds or shades on the wall above the door frame for shape, privacy, and light control. Unify the doors—and disguise the shade or blind headers—by hanging a valance from a pole rod above.

4 MUCH-USED SLIDING DOORS Install stacking panels—the flat fabric panels mount above the doors on a sliding track to follow the natural flow of the sliding door. The visual parallel is striking, while the stack-aside function keeps the decorative treatment practical.

❶ ❷

❸ ❹

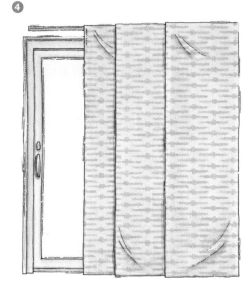

5 SMALL, SQUAT WINDOWS Often positioned high on a basement wall, small rectangular windows can look taller if you hang shutters below. Hang draperies high and wide, exposing as much glass as possible to increase the visual width.

Hang time
Match your curtains' length to your room and style.

The Traditionalist. Measure carefully and have your panels hit exactly at the floor. Weights stitched into a drapery hem help it hang with more heft and keep it in place.

The Casual Spirit. Let curtains lightly skim the bottom of your window frame.

The Hopeless Romantic. Choose extra-long curtains or draperies that puddle on the floor like a ball gown.

The Practicalist. Where privacy and safety are crucial, such as in the kitchen or bath, have curtains graze the windowsill, avoiding unnecessary length that could cause a fire or a fall.

The Minimalist. Opt for crisp wooden shutters. Or adhere frosted decorative window film in a modern, graphic pattern. Shop artists' cooperative websites such as *etsy.com* for affordable artist-designed films.

The Comfort Seeker. Add an extra layer of fabric backing to any curtain or shade for more light control, insulation, privacy, and body.

A well-lit room feels comfy and flatters faces and furnishings. Four expert lighting plans suit your most-used rooms.

Work in layers. A successful lighting plan uses several layers, or types, of illumination. *Ambient*, or overall, indirect light broadly and evenly illuminates rooms. This includes pendants and sconces, as well as overhead fixtures and above-cabinet cove lights that bounce light upward. *Task* light spotlights work areas, including desk and reading lamps and undercounter lights. *Accent* light, such as track lights and adjustable recessed lights, adds depth and dimension while it highlights art and architecture. Add *decorative* light, such as chandeliers and pretty lamps, for sparkle.

SPOTLIGHT ON:
The dining room

Encourage conversation and congeniality by putting your diners in gentle, friendly light. Allow an ❶ overhead fixture, usually a chandelier or a suspended drum pendant, to take center stage, providing the dining room's ambient light. Hang it low enough so the dining table and light seem connected, usually 30 to 36 inches above the tabletop. Accentuate china cabinet walls with ❷ recessed can lights; their lower light levels encourage a relaxed setting, like a cozy bistro. Use ❸ accent lights within glass-front cabinets to highlight stacks of favorite dinnerware. Place ❹ task lamps on sideboards or buffets. Install a master dimmer switch panel to change light and mood levels.

SPOTLIGHT ON:
The living room

From quiet family evenings to ebullient parties, add elements that light the way to comfort. Employ an **1** **overhead fixture** such as a chandelier, to provide ambient light, and bounce light into ceiling corners and areas that task lights such as **2** **table** and **3** **floor lamps** might not reach. Call attention to artwork using simple **4** **ceiling- or wall-mount low-voltage spotlights** or plug-in picture lights. Class up collectibles and books with **5** **petite LEDs** tucked inside a cabinet or display case. Hang mirrors to bounce and bolster the room's light level. Here, too, dimmer switches allow the room's lighting scheme to adapt.

know-how | lighting

SPOTLIGHT ON:

The office

Low lighting and intense glare in a home office strain eyes, cause fatigue, and reduce productivity. These problems are easily addressed. Accent bookshelf and console walls with **1** recessed can lights. Flank a window with a **2** pair of sconces to gently counteract shadows. Avoid harsh glare by choosing fixtures with opaque shades. Spotlight a bulletin board or wall calendar with a **3** strip light installed above, hidden by trim. Create soft, uniform room light by hanging a **4** drum pendant at the room's center. If your desk is also at the center of the room, hang the pendant at a height to enhance your work surface. Highlight bookshelves with **5** puck lights installed at the front of the shelves. A **6** desk lamp with a flexible arm focuses beams down onto your work, not into eyes. Desk placement is key: Control the sunlight hitting your work space by placing the desk with your back to the window and avoid choosing a glossy, reflective surface.

SPOTLIGHT ON:
The kitchen

No one light can provide all the illumination needed in a room, especially the kitchen, which multitasks for cooking, eating, studying, and entertaining. Hang a standout group of **①** **pendant** task lights above the island or kitchen table, slightly higher than eye level, to provide hardworking illumination without glare. Cast light on your work surface with **②** **undercabinet lights** such as puck lights or long strip lights. Banish shadows by installing these task lights at the front of the cabinet (not against the wall), and shield them with trim. Top cabinets with **③** **cove lighting** such as puck or strip lights to fill the room with ambient light. Bouncing light off the ceiling softens shadows on people's faces so they look relaxed. Illuminate the sink area with a **④** **puck or strip light** mounted under a shelf or cornice that spans the adjoining cabinets. Install it on a separate switch for flexibility of use.

know-how | room arranging

Before starting to move those heavy pieces of furniture, settle in and learn the basic floor-plan principles. Here's what to do in four key room types.

FAMILY ROOM

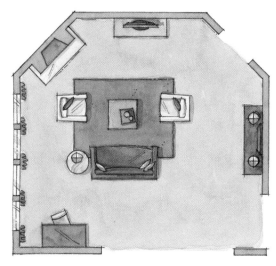

Make room for media
Arrange this casual space for relaxation.

Focus on entertainment. Place the television and computer so the screens face away from sunlight.

Measure up. The viewing distance for a standard TV is 8 to 12 feet. The best viewing angle is not more than 30 degrees.

Manage traffic. For family harmony, create paths that flow behind viewers, not between them and the screen.

Add storage. Consider freestanding pieces in a smaller room and wall-to-wall built-ins in a larger room. Make sure some storage is near the TV.

Opt for multiuse furniture. Options include a sofa bed, chairs on casters, drop-leaf tables, and ottomans that serve as tables or seating.

FAMILY ROOM ONE
One free wall, one wide entry

1 Use an L-shape sectional to focus on both the fireplace and television.

2 Arrange chairs so they don't obstruct traffic flow.

3 Group tables with seating for handy landing spots for drinks and snacks.

4 Choose chairs that swivel to face the sofa, fireplace, or TV.

FAMILY ROOM TWO
One irregular room, one wide traffic lane

1 Use the perimeter of the room for a computer desk and storage console.

2 Choose chairs with casters so they're easy to move.

3 Float the furniture to focus on the fireplace and the television.

4 Group the television and fireplace to keep both visible from every seat.

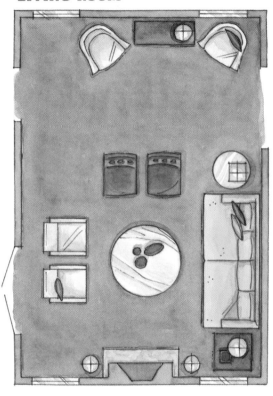

Welcome guests
Adapt the rules to reflect your family's lifestyle.

Face the view. Position the chairs and sofa so they take advantage of the view, whether it's a fireplace, a television, or a window.

Cozy up to talk. For face-to-face chats, place chairs no more than 8 feet apart. In a large room, use furniture to create comfort islands. Face two sofas in the center of a room and group chairs, side tables, and lamps at one end.

Allow for traffic. Allow 30 inches between furniture pieces and 14 to 18 inches between a coffee table and sofa.

Put a table within reach of each seat. Use round pedestal tables as side tables between chairs and sofas. The curves make them easier to maneuver around. When space is tight, use nesting tables.

Wire up. Install in-floor electrical outlets to service floating furniture arrangements.

LIVING ROOM ONE
One long room, entry hall at one end

1 There's no need to crowd; leave room for traffic and an entry drop spot.

2 Cozy key seating pieces up to the fireplace, facing each other.

3 Use end tables as landing spaces on both ends of a long sofa.

4 Pair up chairs to balance the sofa and maximize seating.

LIVING ROOM TWO
No free walls, one centered fireplace

1 Float seating in the center of a room filled with doors and windows.

2 Face chairs and sofa toward each other to encourage conversation.

3 Anchor the conversation grouping with a rug and large coffee table.

4 Frame the space with additional seating and cabinets for storage.

DINING ROOM

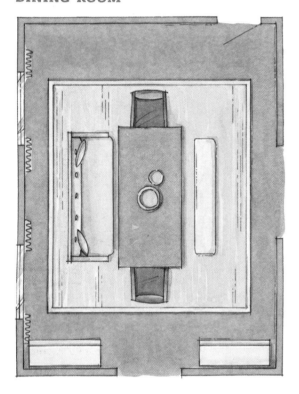

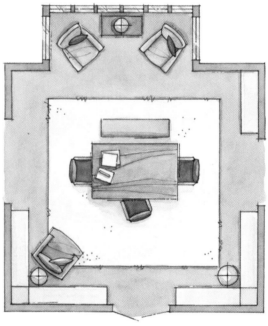

A menu of choices
Maximize a formal dining space.

Consider style. Sit-down meals or buffets? Make furniture choices that support your entertaining style.

Suit the space. Circular tables with pedestal bases let folks see everyone at the table, while rectangular tables limit seating. Allow 20 to 24 inches wide and 15 inches deep per place setting. Leave 6 inches between chairs.

Buy for size. Be sure to allow a minimum of 36 inches from table to wall on all sides. Position the table so traffic flows smoothly around it.

Add function. Make the most of square footage with a wall of shelves that provide storage for the room's alternative uses—office supplies, games, and crafts.

Opt for flexible lighting. Choose and place lighting that adapts to the room's functions. For example, hang the chandelier with extra lengths of cord so it can be adjusted for homework or dining.

DINING ROOM ONE
Rectangular space, no free walls

1 Combine chairs, bench, and settee for an eclectic look.

2 Duplicate the room shape with the table shape to maximize seating.

3 Include storage, such as cabinets or bookcases, on the perimeter.

4 Define the dining space with a rug that contrasts with the flooring.

DINING ROOM TWO
Oversize space/ multiuse space

1 Opt for a table that preserves open space for other uses.

2 Add bookcases to store books, office gear, and tableware.

3 Add chairs for relaxed seating that also can be brought to the table.

4 Anchor the secondary seating areas with lamps and occasional tables.

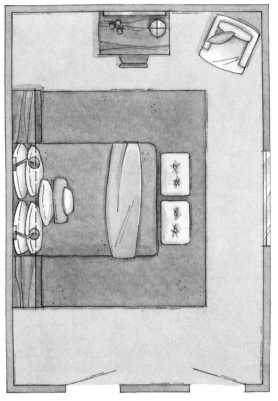

Try this!
Move furniture without any sweat. Log on to *bhg.com* and look in "Tools" for the interactive room-arranging tool.

Relax the bedroom
Start here to create a dreamy spot.

Consider the size of the bed. It's possible to use a larger bed if you don't need a lot of storage furniture. A scroll-like metal headboard consumes less visual space than a solid headboard.

Plan walkways. Allow at least 2 feet on either side for making the bed. Avoid placing the bed within 3 feet of the door; otherwise the bed becomes a roadblock.

Create easy access. Allow 3 feet of dressing space in front of a closet and in front of dressers with drawers.

Adjust for size. In a small bedroom, use fewer pieces of a slightly larger scale to maximize floor space. Opt for tall pieces that add volume in a smaller footprint.

Add comfort. Include a bench at the foot of the bed or a chair and ottoman near a window.

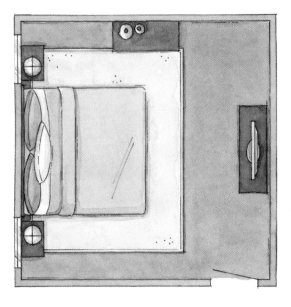

BEDROOM ONE
Long and narrow, one window wall

1 Face the bed to the window to make the most of the view.

2 Include a desk/dressing table, chair, and mirror opposite the doorways.

3 Place a pair of benches at the end of the bed for seating.

4 Nestle a bed into a built-in storage unit that includes two cabinet towers and a cabinet that bridges the head of the bed to create an alcove.

BEDROOM TWO
Square room, two free walls

1 Place the bed so it's the focal point and the room feels grounded.

2 Stretch storage up the wall with a freestanding armoire.

3 Pair matching small-scale dressers to use as nightstands.

4 Position the bed on an oversize rug that allows at least 2 feet on either side and at the foot of the bed.

know-how | flooring

Selecting the right floor covering for your lifestyle and budget means doing some investigative footwork into its hidden features. This chart will save you a few steps.

NAME	CHARACTERISTICS	ADVANTAGES	DISADVANTAGES	CARE
bamboo	Casual, eco-chic look; made from a renewable natural resource; these planks can be nailed, floated, or glued down over most subfloors.	Affordable; durable; some types harder than oak; flame-resistant; naturally moisture-resistant, good choice in humid areas.	Limited, natural palette; fading possible.	Similar to hardwood; consider a home humidifier to maintain a 30 to 50 percent humidity level to avoid shrinking.
cork	Modern look; made from tree bark, a sustainable natural resource; available as glue-down tiles or click-together, laminate-style planks.	Warm, cushiony, and quiet underfoot; can be installed over most preexisting materials; naturally moisture-resistant.	Not for heavy traffic or furnishings—it can dent; limited, natural palette.	Easy upkeep; must be sealed with polyurethane for durability.
laminate	Wide range of colors and patterns, especially popular ones that mimic wood.	More affordable than wood; easier installation; scratch- and stain-resistant; easy to clean and maintain.	Limited to plank form; can't be refinished like wood; can warp from water; can be slippery; may need sound-quieting underlayment.	Easily maintained; avoid wet mopping.
linoleum	Modern and vintage looks; made from renewable, natural resources, including linseed oil.	Durable and quiet; water-resistant; fade-resistant colors; comes in glue-down sheets and tiles, and floating planks; nonallergenic.	Not good for concrete subfloors or wet basements—moisture caught in its underlayment is damaging.	Easy upkeep; must be sealed with polyurethane for durability.
vinyl composition	Made of pressed-vinyl chips, making color solid throughout; originally a commercial product, so very durable.	Durable; colorful; low-cost; low-allergenic.	Available only as tiles; requires polishing for protection, ease of maintenance, and to maintain an attractive appearance.	Damp mop with manufacturer's recommended cleaners.
cushioned sheet vinyl	Wide range of colors, patterns, surface finishes, and prices.	Superior resilience; quiet; comfortable; stain-resistant.	Expensive; lower-cost grades susceptible to nicks and dents.	Easy upkeep with basic cleaners; embossed surfaces trap dirt; most have no-wax features.

NAME	CHARACTERISTICS	ADVANTAGES	DISADVANTAGES	CARE
sheet vinyl	Wide range of colors, patterns, and surface finishes, including ones that mimic natural materials such as wood and stone.	Good resilience; affordable; easy to install and maintain.	Less expensive grades susceptible to nicks and dents; difficult to repair damage.	Easy upkeep with basic cleaners; embossed surfaces trap dirt; most have no-wax features.
solid vinyl tile	Often simulates natural materials such as stone tiles.	Easy-to-install versions, including peel-and-stick; durable; affordable.	Only fair resilience.	Stain-resistant; easy to clean and maintain.
wood	Natural or painted; good selection of looks, plank sizes, and stain colors (if factory-finished) available.	Variety of types and price points, from solid hardwood to more-affordable engineered woods; good resilience; can be refinished; resists spills, scratches, and wear if sealed properly.	Softer woods are less durable than hardwood counterparts; does not reduce noise.	Should be sealed with polyurethane to resist water damage; manufactured floors usually are presealed; use cleaners that don't leave a residue.
brick, slate, quarry tile	Natural, earthy look; variety of shapes.	Durable; beautiful; hard surface won't trap bacteria or dust mites.	No resilience; may require specialized installation.	Slate and quarry tile may need sealer; good stain resistance.
ceramic tile	Colorful; abundant shapes and designs available.	Beautiful; durable; low-maintenance; glazed tiles are good for moisture-prone, heavy-traffic areas and are stain- and fade-resistant.	No resilience; cold underfoot; noisy under hard-soled shoes; grout lines must be resealed periodically.	Clean with soap and water only.
marble	Costly; available as slab or tiles.	Sophisticated look; variety of natural colors based on where it was quarried.	Hard, cold underfoot; noisy under hard-soled shoes; stains and scratches easily.	Needs waxing; stains are difficult to remove.
granite, limestone	Natural look.	Superhard surface won't trap dust mites or bacteria; granite can be "flamed" for slip-resistance; limestone can be tumbled for an intentionally worn look.	Can stain, so consider a professional sealer; no resilience; hard and cold underfoot; noisy under hard-soled shoes; can scratch, so use furniture pads.	Abrasive grit can be damaging—vacuum on a gentle, no-bristle setting; damp mop with a gentle no-detergent, no-acid cleaner.

Nothing beats carpet for its wealth of styles and wiggle-your-toes comfort. It's also the highest-maintenance flooring, so consider wear and stains before you buy.

NAME	CHARACTERISTICS	ADVANTAGES	DISADVANTAGES	CARE
cotton	Soft fiber used for informal area or scatter rugs.	Comfortable underfoot.	Limited durability.	Cleans very well; some rugs machine-washable.
wool	Deep, warm, rich look—the fiber synthetics try to match for its natural beauty.	Easily dyed; renewable resource; stain-resistant.	Can be expensive; limited durability; must be treated to repel stains and resist static electricity.	Not as easy to clean as many synthetic fibers.
jute and sisal	Used for informal matting; available mostly in earth tones; can be painted or stenciled.	Affordable; offer textural contrast; relax formal rooms; renewable resource.	Fair-to-poor durability and resistance to wear and soil; not as soft underfoot as conventional carpet.	Not easily cleaned; shed fibers.
acrylic	Closest synthetic fiber to wool; low-allergenic; resists mildew, moths, and dust mites; comes in a range of colors.	Moderate price; crush-resistant; springy; fade-resistant; generates minimal static electricity.	May pill; not as resilient, durable, or stain-resistant as wool or nylon.	Cleans very well; smooth fibers resist soil.
nylon	The most popular fiber; wide selection of colors and textures.	Moderate price; soft, resilient; strongest synthetic fiber; good color retention; resists mildew and shedding.	Static-prone in forced-air heated homes unless treated; cut-filament loop carpet may pill.	Good cleanability.
polyester	Similar to wool in look and feel; some fibers made from recycled plastic bottles.	Less expensive than nylon or wool; resilient; abrasion- and static-resistant; sheds moisture.	Does not wear as well as wool or nylon; some pilling and shedding; susceptible to oil-base stains.	Good cleanability, enhanced by stain-resistant treatments.
olefin/ polypropylene	Synthetic fiber in primarily loop and randomly sheared textures; can be used in indoor-outdoor rooms.	Moderate price; nonabsorbent; resists stains, abrasion, static, pilling, shedding; fibers can withstand moisture.	Least bouncy underfoot; lower grades may crush or flatten.	Excellent cleanability.

Adaptable area rugs

Use rugs to shape and enhance your floor plan. In a foyer with high traffic flow, use a washable or **1** indoor-outdoor runner to lead your eye into the rest of your home. In a living room, place furniture around the room's centerpiece such as a fireplace. If the area rug is neutral, layer a small patterned or **2** colorful rug under a coffee table. Choose a **3** square rug large enough for all the furniture legs to rest on and to anchor the seating area. In the dining room, select a **4** rug to accentuate the shape of the dining table (here, it's round); the legs of all seating need to sit well within the area rug. A busy **5** back entry or a **6** kitchen with lots of spills might benefit from carpet tiles that are easily removed for hosing off to clean, or replaced if badly stained. If rugs are visible through multiple rooms, have a common color in each of the **7** rugs to tie them together. In a bedroom with low-pile, **8** wall-to-wall carpeting, use a colorful **9** patterned rug to delineate a dressing space or seating area.

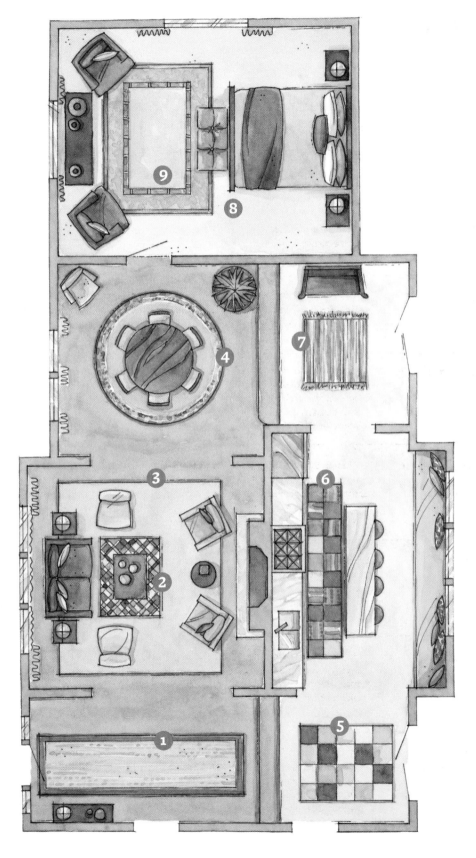

Learn how to buy the perfect piece of furniture at the perfect price.

BUY SMART

Do your homework. "Shop" magazines and catalogs first. Focus on furniture scaled to the room size. Study photos of rooms to spy a look you like, then copy the scale of the pieces. Look for bargains at outlet stores and closeout sections in furniture stores. Always ask if the retailer has a better price.

Measure up. Create a floor plan so you know what will fit. Make sure the furniture can be moved through the front door or up the stairs.

Choose right. Buy what you love and what works with what you own. Coordinate styles that complement rather than match, such as a boxy sofa with a side table with curvy legs. For big, expensive items, opt for neutral finishes that offer long-term appeal and versatility.

GET STARTED

Eye it. Stand 15 feet from a sofa or chair and look for pleasing proportions and well-matched fabric. Then check for straight welting, corners with flat seams, and a ripple-free back.

Sit a spell. Note the depth of the seat and the height and pitch of the back—the three biggest comfort factors. Eight-way, hand-tied springs make up the strongest support system; less expensive sinuous steel springs are a solid alternative. The seat should offer gentle support and rise with you as you stand. Look for durable polyurethane cushions (density rating of 1.8 to 2.5). Unzip the cushion and look for a muslin cover that keeps the cushion stable. If you find that it's stuffed with batting or shredded foam, walk away—the sofa will become a lumpy mess.

Check the frame. Look for a frame of solid kiln-dried hardwood or semi-hardwood 1½ inches thick, and joints that are screwed and glued together. Make sure stress points (near the legs and center) are supported with corner blocks. Give the sofa a light shake to make sure it's sturdy, and lift one end; it should be heavy.

Finish with fabric. Tightly woven fabrics wear better than looser weaves. Stain-resistant synthetics, such as microfiber or nylon, are options for family room furniture. Leather, chenille, or silk blends cost more. Fabric grades indicate different price levels, not durability.

Piece by piece
Use furniture to make a room stylish and livable.

Plan for function. Select a simple grouping of furniture pieces that work toward the room's purpose—dining, sleeping, working, or relaxing. Eliminate extraneous pieces.

Go bold. Choose one or two focal-point furniture pieces to deliver style punch and a designer focus to the room.

Direct traffic. Consider how to move people through a room. Eliminate traffic blockades by substituting movable occasional tables for a too-large coffee table or a sleek sectional for two bulky sofas. Create an easy path that avoids interrupting conversations or television viewing.

Think outside the set. Acquire furniture one piece at a time rather than buying matched sets that often create inflexible arrangements. Choose pieces in a compatible style so you can move them from room to room.

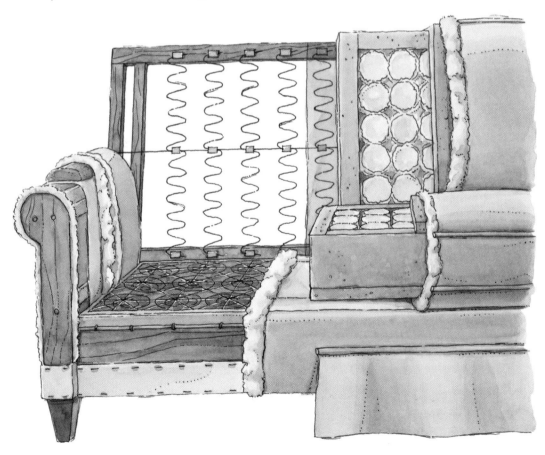

Seat yourself comfortably on the perfectly stylish sofa or chair.

SOFA AND CHAIR STYLES

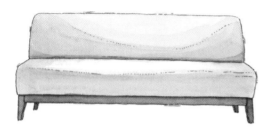

TIGHT BACK, TIGHT SEAT Crisp and modern, this silhouette mixes with many styles. It's comfy for small spaces and cocktail-party perches but not for lounging.

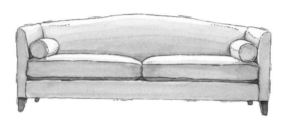

TIGHT BACK, LOOSE SEAT, MULTICUSHION Balance comfort with soft seating and a firm back. Cushions can be flipped for even wear.

TUFTED, SINGLE CUSHION This elegant silhouette with high arms has clubby appeal. A single sofa cushion comfortably seats more people.

LOOSE BACK, LOOSE SEAT, MULTICUSHION Modular pieces offer style and flexibility. Loose cushions on seat and back offer the most comfort. Buy better-quality cushions that keep their shape.

TIGHT BACK, LOOSE SEAT Double the wear of the seat with a loose cushion that's easy to flip. A tight back offers a classic profile.

TUFTED BACK AND SEAT Tufted back, arms, and seat offer a traditional silhouette. Tufting adds elegance to solid fabrics and leathers.

Leather or not?
Learn the basics before you buy.

Grade it. Leather grades indicate durability and price. Look for top-grain leather from the outer surface of the hide. Split-grain leathers are taken from lower surfaces and are much weaker. Top-grain hides become soft and supple with use.

Finish matters. Top-grain leather is sold in three finishes: aniline, semi-aniline, and pigmented. Aniline leather is soaked in transparent aniline dye, but does not have other finishes or pigments applied. Only about 5 percent of hides are perfect enough to become anilines. Semi-aniline leathers have a small amount of coating or pigment added to even out the color and offer protection against stains and fading. Pigmented leathers, sometimes called painted leathers, are fully treated with surface color and are stiffer than anilines.

DINING ROOM CHAIR STYLES

MIDCENTURY MODERN CHAIR A streamlined shape of molded plywood plus chrome legs offers the best of modern simplicity. Pair it with a worn wood table.

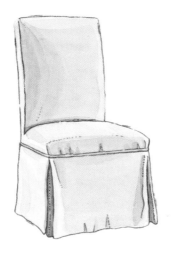

PARSONS CHAIR The chameleon of the dining room, the Parsons chair reflects a modern or traditional attitude depending on the fabric and style of slipcover.

FRENCH OVAL-BACK SIDE CHAIR Use this pretty chair with other styles for an eclectic approach. Cover the seat and back with stain-resistant fabric.

WING CHAIR Curvy shoulders and a cinched waist give this host chair lasting appeal. Upholster it in rich fabric to accent the sinewy lines.

RUSH-SEAT CHAIR A ladder-back chair with a rush seat offers comfort and character. Paint the frame a bright hue for modern appeal.

WINDSOR CHAIR History comes to the table in this version with a spindle back and continuous horseshoe arm. This classic style is surprisingly comfortable.

Eco wise

Keeping your design Earth-friendly is easier and more stylish than ever.

Redo and renew. Updating existing furniture is one way to be an eco-friendly decorator. After all, a new coat of no-VOC paint may be all it takes to freshen a table or chairs, while reupholstering a sofa or chair keeps it out of the landfill. Plus, you get to save a favorite piece. Selecting organic fabrics for the redo is a planet-friendly option.

Buy eco-new. Many manufacturers offer planet-friendly furniture. Look for cushions made from soy-base foam and covered with organic or natural fabrics, pillows made from 100-percent-recycled fibers, frames crafted from wood certified by the Forest Stewardship Council and Sustainable Forestry Initiative (SFI), and water-base finishes.

know-how | buying tips

Find the right tables to serve leading and supporting roles in living and dining rooms.

DINING TABLES

ROUND PEDESTAL TABLE The star of tight dining quarters, the center pedestal makes it easy to take your seat, while the round top welcomes more diners than a square one.

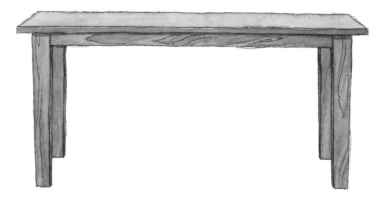

RECTANGULAR TABLE Perfect in a rectangular dining room, this table comes in a variety of lengths and widths to suit your needs. Perfect for two host chairs at the ends and any number of chairs along each side.

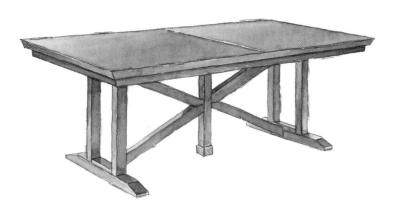

TRESTLE TABLE The base adds flexibility to a rectangular top because the legs allow diners to sit just about anywhere.

PEDESTAL TABLE WITH LEAF An added leaf makes this oval table suitable for a rectangular dining room and plenty of guests. Remove the leaf to make it a round table for intimate dinners.

ACCENT TABLES

OVAL COFFEE TABLE Eases traffic through a room with its cornerless shape. Provides storage below deck.

NESTING TABLES These small-space wonders offer a compact silhouette that expands as needed.

QUALITY CHECKLIST

1 Take a look
To assess the quality of furniture, first consider the materials. Solid hardwoods (such as maple, oak, and walnut) and softwood pines (pine, spruce) are the most durable. Many quality pieces are built from veneers (thin sheets of wood over less expensive plywood). Beware of cheap plywood versions that can be flimsy and chip easily.

2 Check the joints
Well-made case goods are joined with dovetails, screws, and wood blocks—not staples or nails, which become loose over time. Mortise-and-tenon joinery also creates strong joints without interrupting the design, a necessity for pieces that get heavy use.

3 Test how it works
Slide drawers in and out to ensure they glide easily. Drawers with rollers and glides on each side are best; one center bottom roller and glide is OK for light use. Drawer stops prevent accidentally pulling all the way out. Doors should swing easily without squeaking or rubbing. Check movable shelves to be sure they're tight and secure and slide in and out with ease. Make sure table leaves fit securely.

4 Consider stability
Top-heavy pieces may topple over when filled with heavy objects such as books. Secure these pieces to the wall. Large, tall pieces often come with hardware to attach them to the wall. Look for adjustable feet for uneven floors and hidden casters for moving heavy pieces.

dovetail

mortise and tenon

Table talk
Choose tables that handle what life dishes out.

Be flexible. Consider a drop-leaf table that expands for company or small accent tables to replace a large coffee table to open up more floor space.

Check the finish. Glossy sheens and dark stains or paint show nicks faster, while light woods and distressed finishes disguise blemishes. Ask about watertight coatings to avoid water rings. If you have children, skip glass tops in favor of a scratch-resistant finish.

Test it. Make sure the dining table has enough elbowroom, ideally about 30 inches between chair centers. Lean on the table to check for wobbling. See if you can sit at the table and cross your legs. Check that the chairs, including arms, fit under the table edge.

Put it to work. Look for coffee or end tables with shelves or drawers to add storage.

tips we love | shopping

Make smart shopping and budgeting choices for your home with our expert tips.

EDITOR'S FAVORITE
Keep a list of specific items you're looking for. It'll help you shop sales for what you really need rather than being distracted by what you don't.

"Time your makeover when things go on sale, usually the end of the summer or end of winter. It makes redecorating attainable and affordable."
—**Annette Joseph,** interior designer

"Swap out pillows and throws for ones in a new color or fresh texture. You'll get great visual punch in a room without spending a lot."
—**Elaine Griffin,** interior designer

"Rearrange your furniture. It's free. Pull out all of the knickknacks and small pieces first, then reposition the large furniture. Add back only the items you truly love."
—**Janna A. Lufkin,** interior designer

"Shop consignment stores. They usually take only high-quality items and upholstered pieces are typically in excellent condition. And the price drops dramatically the longer an item sits on the floor."

—**Matthew Mead,** stylist

"Buy from hotel surplus stores— check the Yellow Pages under 'hotel surplus.' "

—**Meredith Drummond,** author

EDITOR'S FAVORITE
Shop your cupboards for items you no longer use but can repurpose as decorative organizers. A small bowl, for instance, makes a pretty organizer on a desk, dresser, or nightstand.

"A reversible bedspread gives two looks for the price of one."

—**Jean Norman,** author

what month does it go on sale?

JANUARY Carpet & Flooring	**MAY THROUGH AUGUST** Mattresses
MARCH, SEPTEMBER China & Flatware	**SUMMER** Paint
MAY, JUNE, DECEMBER Cookware	**AFTER LABOR DAY** Patio Furniture
OCTOBER, NOVEMBER Dining Furniture	**DECEMBER** Small Appliances
JANUARY, JULY, HOLIDAY WEEKENDS Furniture	**EARLY SPRING, ALSO SIX TO 12 MONTHS AFTER A PARTICULAR MODEL IS LAUNCHED** Televisions
JANUARY Linens	

ADDITIONAL NEW IMAGE CREDITS

page 33
Field editor and stylist, Sandi Mohlmann.
Designer, Kathryn Chaplow. Architect,
Jeff Visser.

pages 168–173
Field editor and stylist: Brice Gaillard.
Designer, Michelle Prentice. Architect,
Allison Ramsey.

pages 200–203
Field editor and stylist: Andrea Caughey.
Designer, Cher Beall.

pages 212–217
Field editor and stylist: Mona Dworkin.
Designer, Jenny Andrews. Architect, Jay
Hugo.